CW00602887

Molly Benjamin is the founder of Ladies Finance Club in Australia and the UK, which brings women together to learn about money in a fun and social environment (without the boring bits). Ladies Finance Club has had over 35,000 women through their programs, workshops, courses and membership!

GIRLS JUST WANNA HAVE FUNDS

MOLLY BENJAMIN

I acknowledge and pay respect to the land and waterways of the traditional Aboriginal families of the Gadigal people of the Eora Nation, where this book was written, and their Elders both past and present.

Always was, always will be Aborginal land.

First published by Affirm Press in 2023
Boon Wurrung Country
28 Thistlethwaite Street
South Melbourne VIC 3205
affirmpress.com.au

10 9 8 7 6 5 4 3 2 1

A catalogue record for this book is available from the National Library of Australia

ISBN: 9781922806376 (flexi-bound)

Cover and internal design by Emily Thiang © Affirm Press
Cover image by Monica Pronk Photography
Typeset in Avenir
Printed and bound in China by C&C Offset Printing

To your new money journey!

I hope this book gets you to a place where ordering extra guacamole won't be a big financial decision and you can cruise the Med with your gal pals in retirement.

Contents

Introduction

So you want to get your money shit together or perhaps you've got it together (go you!) and want to get to the next level. Career-wise, things might be pretty good, you've got some fab stuff in your wardrobe and you're all about brunch and international (*cough*, domestic) travel. But somewhere inside that little voice is starting to speak up about taking more control of your cash. Maybe it all seems a bit hard or a bit boring – a 'future you' problem.

But there's a reason you've picked up this book, and I have a sneaking little suspicion it might be for some of the following reasons:

- You're sick of feeling out of control with money.
- You want a plan for your debt.
- You dream of owning a house … one day.
- You want to grow your money through investing.
- You want to have 'enough' for retirement but are not sure what 'enough' is.
- You want to teach your kids good financial habits that you were never taught (or your super cute, hypothetical children).
- You want to get to the point where adding guacamole isn't a big financial decision.
- All of the above.

Or perhaps this book was shoved into your hands by a well-meaning, slightly passive-aggressive family member who said, '*Read this*, you need it!' Whatever the reason, I am glad you're here.

Confession: I was really bad with money. I would have preferred to get a Brazilian wax than create a budget. My investments were made up of clothes and #GoodTimes! I was a financial mess. I had been working in the corporate world for years with nothing to show but an empty savings account. Every time I would try to get my head around 'my money', there was so much jargon I had no idea where to begin, and so I didn't. I just delayed and delayed until I realised something had to change.

I also started to realise I wasn't alone. One Sunday, after a particularly fun weekend, my girlfriends and I were talking about how broke we all were #YOLO. It had almost become a joke.

'I'm sooooo broke.'

'No, I'm so broke.'

I said, 'Wait a minute, we all earn pretty good money yet we're all living payday to payday. What's going on?'

Even the women I worked with (and I was literally working for a bank) were a bit clueless when it came to their personal finances. But it felt like many of my guy mates were building their investment portfolios and getting into the property market. Why were we so far behind? When were we supposed to get our money shit together? I was almost 30, surely it should have happened by now. Did I miss the memo?

The more I researched women and money, the more alarmed I became.

I learnt that:

- Women live on average five years longer than men.
- We earn less (14.7% pay gap made worse by Covid).
- We retire with 42% less super.

- Almost half of all women (41%) find money decisions overwhelming and stressful.
- ASIC found that almost all women (85%) under 35 don't understand investment concepts.
- Women over the age of 55 are the fastest-growing group to experience homelessness.

I didn't want to become one of the statistics, and I didn't want my sisters, my friends or their mums to become one either. I didn't want that for any woman. I wanted to do something about it.

So I took matters into my own hands. Five of my girlfriends came over to my house and we ordered some pizzas, poured wine and invited a mate's friend who worked in finance to teach us about this 'finance stuff'. I was worried it might be a bit awkward, but it wasn't. We had so many questions and there was such a hunger in the room to understand. We finally had permission to discuss money and, my gosh, did it feel good. Word got out about our little finance rendezvous and more and more friends wanted in. We quickly outgrew my living room. Having worked in communications and events my whole career, I thought, 'Why don't I open the event up and see who would like to come?'

I ran my first event in London and it sold out in a week. And so the Ladies Finance Club was born.

Since that first event we have spoken to over 20,000 women about money. We have run events with women from Microsoft, Google, Pinterest, Deloitte and now have hundreds of members in Australia and in the UK who we are helping get fierce with their finances. We work with the best experts in the finance game to break down the topic of money.

But nothing has made me more proud than the stories I hear of women changing their lives after joining our club or coming along to an event. For one of our members, having money meant she could leave a relationship that turned abusive and controlling, and set up a new life.

For another, money meant she could freeze her eggs and buy herself more time to have a child and find a partner; another wrote to me and said she now wasn't going to retire into poverty having learnt to contribute more to her super fund.

I have met women at Ladies Finance Club who had no idea about investing and now call ETFs their best friends (don't worry if you're like WTF is an ETF – all will be revealed). I have seen women get out of credit card debt using the method we talk you through in this book. I know women whose retirements are going to look hundreds of thousands of dollars different because they took charge now!

And the great news is women are really good at money! Research shows that we make great investors and savers when we have a goal and a plan in place. In Australia, women are more likely to own their own home and pay it off than our male counterparts.

> 'Money can't buy happiness, but it can make you awfully comfortable while you're being miserable.'
>
> Clare Booth Luce, American writer

It's easier than you think

Getting your finance shit together is so much easier than people make out. I honestly thought it would mean no fun or social activities, taking depressing-looking sandwiches to work, writing down every dollar I spent on a scary spreadsheet and that it would take forever to get to the point where I could invest. But I didn't need to make any huge dramatic changes to my life. I could still eat out, I could still travel, I could still do all the things I did before, plus I felt way more in control and way less guilty when I did spend. And it turned out I didn't need to wait to invest anyway, because I could get started with just $50.

If I can do it, you can do it

I ran into an old roommate who laughed in my face when I said I was writing a book on finance (I know right, *rude*) but I couldn't blame him – if you had seen me in my early twenties you would be like, 'Biatch, please'. I was the last person who ever thought I would write a book on the topic of finance.

But if I can get my money shit together, you definitely can do it as well. Being good with money doesn't have anything to do with being a maths whiz. If you can do grade three maths you've got what it takes to #NailThis. Being good with money has a lot more to do with your mindset, beliefs and behaviours (and you're going to learn all about those in this book).

Grab your gal pals

Like all journeys, it's better with gal pals, and snacks (and prosecco or non-alcoholic options of course). The whole concept of Ladies Finance Club is that you do it with friends – we are bringing each other on this journey, creating a community and a movement of money-savvy women. Plus, doing it with a gal pal makes it more fun and increases the chances that you'll follow through. And if you want to be cruising around the Mediterranean on a yacht with your gal pals in your eighties they are going to need money as well!

How to use this book

Step 1: You can totally do this by yourself, but if you want some accountability we recommend you create a WhatsApp Group or Facebook Group – feel free to name it your own Ladies Finance Club. If your friends are a bit reluctant, jump on our Facebook group, 'Ladies Finance Club – Money Chat!', and find someone to do it with or join Ladies Finance Club's membership.

Step 2: At the end of each chapter, there are actions for you all to take to keep each other accountable (don't worry – they are small actions). You have my permission to peer pressure each other into taking action to help you set up a strong financial future.

Step 3: Set up a time once a month where you can come together and chat through each chapter.

Don't compare and despair

If you're in a really different place financially from your friends, it's easy to compare, but that's not what we are about. We are all on our own journey, so whether you're building your emergency fund, getting out of 'Buy Now Pay Later' debt or looking to buy your first home or investments, you're in a safe place.

We have three rules at LFC

1 The First Rule of Ladies Finance Club is we do talk about finance

We talk about it to all the women in our lives – our mum, sisters, friends, work wives, cousins, that random chick you do yoga with! Money is something we use every day, so let's not be scared to talk about it. Find out how the people in your life budget, how they negotiate and what they are investing in or saving for – it needs to stop being taboo.

2 You are the only one responsible for your money

We can't rely on rich uncles, inheritances, winning the lotto or marrying a prince (there are not many single ones left – I checked). It's very easy to hand your financial power over to your partner 'cause you're a busy lady but no one is going to care about your money situation as much as you. If you haven't been the one making the money moves then let this be your call-up. Be your own knight in shining armour.

3 There are no 'dumb' questions

Like me, you probably missed the Money 101 lesson in school (because it didn't exist). We have never learnt about this before so be gentle with yourself. If you're struggling, connect with our community.

And just for the record, I am not a millionaire (yet) and I don't own property at the time of writing this book – I am currently saving for my first property. I'm just a girl who was really bad at money who got way better at it, built an emergency fund and investment portfolio, and who has a special knack for taking complex ideas and breaking them down into something that actually makes sense. I am not a financial advisor (phew) and as I don't hold a financial licence nothing in this book should be taken as financial advice. I'll just be sharing tips and tools that have helped me and other women at Ladies Finance Club.

I want this to be a really practical guide and I have reached out to some of my favourite women and Ladies Finance Club ambassadors – who are experts in the areas of finance, debt, family law and tax – and combined it with some of my own learnings to make it bite-sized and actionable, designed not to overwhelm but to empower you. It's the book I wish I'd had in my twenties.

I've also included a list of useful tools and resources at the back of the book, many of which can be found at ladiesfinanceclub.com.money, to make things easier for you as you go on your money journey.

The exciting thing is that when women are financially empowered they can change the world. They create better lives for their families, community and the environment. They give more to charity (hello, MacKenzie Scott, who after splitting with Jeff Bezos has given away over $12 billion). We also know it's young female investors who are driving the shift to sustainable investments, which is a game changer for our planet.

It's an exciting time to be a woman. Never before have we earned so much money and had this level of control and power over our lives (in first world countries). Women are becoming an economic force, with women controlling a third of the world's wealth and adding $5 trillion to the wealth pool globally every year.

In Australia we make up more than 50% of the population – imagine if we controlled 50% of its wealth.

It's an exciting time, so let's get money savvy. You can totally do this!

Big love,

Molly xxx

CHAPTER 1

Your Money Mindset

Did you know that your money habits are largely formed by the time you are seven years old? YIKES!

Way back when you were trading Tazos, feeding your Tamagotchi or playing with your Bratz dolls, you were locking in the money habits that would stay with you into adult life.

In this chapter, I'm going to help you identify your money mindset and some of the money blocks that might be holding you back so you can hold onto the good and say sayonara to the bad.

What is a money mindset?

Your money mindset is your set of beliefs around money (usually subconscious). It's how we feel about money and it affects how much we will make and keep in our life.

Where does your money mindset come from?

A range of different factors go into the mixing pot that makes up our money mindset. A few include:

- **How our parents behaved and talked (or didn't talk) about money.** Who heard their parents say the classic line, 'Money doesn't grow on trees' or 'We can't afford that'? Or did they teach you that 'Money is abundant' and 'You can always make more'? Did you see your parents work really hard to earn money so you now think that you have to work really hard to make money as well?
- **Whether people argued about money in your family.** If you grew up with parents fighting about money you might have beliefs around it being a bad thing and be self-sabotaging yourself by spending and giving away your money.

- **If you grew up feeling wealthy or poor.** This isn't actually about whether you were rich or poor but how you felt. One of our members, Jess, grew up in a very wealthy family and she never took money seriously as she hadn't ever worried about it but now she struggles with managing it. Whereas another member, Leah, grew up in a family where things felt very tight, and there were always stressful conversations about money so she's very careful with her spending and feels guilty for what she has.
- **The financial climate you grew up in.** Where you grew up has an impact on your beliefs around money. For example, one of my former colleagues grew up in communist Poland and another grew up in a city in America where heaps of people lost their jobs during the global financial crisis – these factors impacted their relationship with money (and fair enough).
- **The culture you grew up in.** If money was looked after by one particular gender in your family, or if it was rude to talk about money, this also has an impact on your money beliefs.

I have talked to hundreds of women about money and it's quite common that we didn't receive positive messages about money from our parents (and chances are our parents didn't receive positive messages about money from their parents either).

At a recent conference, successful business author Andrew Griffiths was retelling a story where another speaker showed kids an image of a large pile of cash and asked them what this meant to them. The kids yelled out words like 'fighting', 'guilt', 'selfishness', 'arguing'. There were no shouts of 'opportunity' and 'freedom'; the children all had negative associations with money, which would have been shaped by their parents. Isn't that wild?

Your money story

Knowing your money story is really important. It allows you to understand the way you interact and think about money, and how to change it (if need be). It can be helpful to take a trip down memory lane to remember what those cringe-worthy haircuts and early memories were teaching you.

Ask yourself (or discuss with your gal pal):

- What is my earliest memory of money?
- Growing up did I feel rich or poor?
- How did it feel to earn money for the first time?
- What money lessons did my parents teach me?
- How was money discussed at home?
- Who looked after the money growing up: Mum or Dad? Why?

Is there any correlation between your early money habits or memories and how you are acting with money now?

Money personality

Identifying your money personality helps you to understand yourself better, particularly around the way you approach things like spending, saving or investing. By understanding it, you can then take action to change it. Just don't use it as an excuse as to why you can't get better with money – 'Oh I'm such a spendthrift, it's just my personality'.

Read the following money personalities and look at who rings most true for you.

Amanda

Amanda is a yes gal. Her money brings her joy and she loves treating herself and the people she loves. When she gets money she spends it.

If an unexpected bill pops up she relies on her credit card. She keeps meaning to build up her emergency fund but hasn't gotten around to it. She finds it difficult to put aside money for long-term financial goals because there never seems to be anything left at the end of the month.

Jenna

As soon as Jenna gets paid she puts her savings away. Her emergency fund is full and she can't understand why anyone would want a credit card (unless for reward points). She feels guilty when she spends money on herself and doesn't like that sometimes her siblings ask her for money. She is saving for a house and has to think hard before she spends any money. She'd like to start investing but is worried she might lose money. For Jenna, money means security and control.

Lui

Lui doesn't know exactly how much she spends each month and her financial situation is a bit all over the place. She hates the thought of doing a budget. She's always scrambling to get her tax done on time and just crosses her fingers and hopes for the best. She forgets to open bills and has been known to pay late fees. She wishes she didn't have to think about it. Adulting is hard enough.

Pip

Pip loves a bargain and is a savvy shopper! She is happiest when there is a large balance in her bank account and she has money to spend, save or invest. If her bank account looks low, she feels like she has failed. She has been known to say 'No' to things she actually wanted to do because they seemed like a waste of money at the time. She's got a solid emergency fund now and loves investing and seeing her money grow. She's someone who seeks the best tax advice at tax time. And she is thinking about contributing more to her super fund so she can set herself up for retirement now.

Aisha

Aisha lives simply and doesn't really feel like she needs that much money because there are more important things in life. She's generous with friends and always the first to offer to 'pay for coffee'. If an emergency happens she would probably just reach out to family and friends to see if they could help. Aisha rarely buys expensive things and loves a good vintage shop. On payday, she feels uneasy when her bank account is full and she worries that lots of money will turn her into a greedy or selfish person.

Who do you identify with the most?

Amanda – The Spender

Money encourages you to enjoy and live in the moment.

Let's bring in some balance.

1. Set up automatic payments so on payday, before you pay any bills or treat yourself, you pay yourself first (more on this in Chapter 2).
2. Write down everything you spend for a week and rank each thing from one to ten for enjoyment and value.
3. For each purchase, work out your hourly rate and how much time it would take you to pay for it. Then wait 24 hours before buying so you can think about whether you really need this or you're just impulse buying.

Jenna – The Saver

Money helps you achieve your goals.

Let's bring some joy back to money!

1. Start a fun money fund – money that is just spent on things that bring you joy!
2. Learn about growing your wealth through investing.
3. Look at your goals. Are they what you really want to achieve or are they someone else's goals?

Lui – The Avoider

Money isn't a priority, you just like to go with the flow.

Let's start getting an understanding of where our money is going.

1. Work out what your essentials (living expenses) are.
2. Download a budgeting app (see our resources page) so you can see what you are spending.
3. Challenge yourself to look at your bank account each day.

Pip – The Accumulator

Money helps you feel in control and secure.

Let's start enjoying our money!

1. Don't budget the fun out of life – put money aside for gifts.
2. Give yourself a break. Put money aside for a fun holiday.
3. Schedule in activities that you love doing once a month.

Aisha – The Money Monk

Money helps you feel good by giving to others.

Let's start looking after you!

1. Write a list of why money is good.
2. Negotiate your salary if you haven't in a while (see Chapter 13).
3. Look at investing in ethical options that align with your values.

Money beliefs

The messages you tell yourself about money matter and shape your behaviour.

You might not think of money as an emotional issue, but most people have really strong emotional attachments to money, even if they don't realise it.

Leading money mindset and financial coach trainer Simonne Gnessen asked LFC members on a coaching call to imagine if money came to their house for tea:

- What would it look like?
- How would you feel seeing it?
- Would you let it in?

It's a great exercise to reveal your unconscious thoughts and messages about money.

Some common beliefs we hear that can hold women back include:

- I can either do what I love or make money.
- I don't make enough money to save.
- Money will make me evil.
- Money makes people fight.
- Making money is really hard.

Write down your own negative money blocks (or use any of the above if you believe them).

Shift your money mindset

Caroline Brewin, Director of Brain Powered Coaching, says, 'You have the power to shape your mindset – it's a choice you can make every day ... Just decide who and how you want to be and you'll carve that vision and pathway for your life.'

Let's take the example of buying a house.

Belief: I'm never going to be able to afford a house.

Your brain will look for evidence: 'Oh yes, houses are so expensive, everyone says it's not a good time.'

Actions: Well, we won't do anything.

Result: No home.

Let's shift that belief!

Belief: I will be able to afford a house.

Your brain will look for evidence: 'I can access the first-home buyer's grant and houses are for sale everywhere.'

Actions: You will start a house fund, speak to a mortgage broker, start going to inspections.

Result: You buy a home.

Upgrade your money mindset

I want to be super upfront. Being 'good at money' is about behaviour and habits, not about how intelligent you are! As they say, it's not your salary habits that make you rich but your spending habits. I have met air hostesses who are on a moderate salary but have investment portfolios, and I have met high-level executives who are in serious credit card debt.

People think having more money means you will be better at money, but the reality is if you can't look after $1000, you won't be able to look after $10,000 or $1 million. That's why lotto winners frequently lose their money and celebrities end up bankrupt – because they haven't done the mindset work.

I'm still amazed at what a taboo talking about money is. I know more intimate and graphic details of my girlfriends' sex lives (who doesn't love an oversharer?) than I do about their money situation. We spend zero time talking about if they invest, how they budget and what they are saving for. According to a Merrill study, 61% of women would rather talk about their own death than money. That's grim.

Sydney based financial advisor Jessica Brady, from Fox and Hare Financial Advice and Ladies Talk Money, shared some interesting research with LFC members that looked at financial literacy, confidence and competency within men and women.

Men scored higher than women when they rated how confident they felt with money; however, from a competency perspective, women and men were the same. Jess says, 'It's just that most guys think they understand more about financial stuff (they talk about it with their mates), and so the ladies think, "Well, he seems to get it more than I do, best leave it to him," so they let their male partners look after the money and then it becomes a self-fulfilling prophecy where the guys are doing it more, so then they are learning more, and get better at it!'

The takeaway point is: if you don't feel confident right now, that doesn't mean you aren't competent. You can do this!

How can I change my mindset?

The great news is you can totally reset your money mindset. A study by financial expert Chris Hogan of over 10,000 millionaires found that 97% of them believed that they could become millionaires. What you believe will drive your behaviour, which will lead to positive results.

So how do we change our beliefs around money?

Forgive yourself

A great starting point is to forgive yourself for past money mistakes. Recognise that you were doing the best you could with the information you had at the time then say the simple phrase, 'I forgive myself for my money pasts.'

Unblock negative money beliefs

Write down your negative money beliefs and think about what thoughts, emotions and memories come up. If a belief doesn't make sense, what would be a better and more empowering belief to have?

THE LANGUAGE WE USE AROUND MONEY MATTERS!	
Instead of this	**Try this**
I'm terrible with money	I'm learning how to manage my money
We can't afford that	Let's start saving for that
I'll never be out of debt	I have a plan of action and will take it one day at a time
I'm never going to understand investing, why bother?	I'll start by watching LFCs investing 101 videos this weekend (with a glass of wine)
I don't earn enough money to save	I'm grateful I can cover my bills, I'm going to save 10% of my next pay

#Gratitude

I know #Gratitude and #Grateful are buzzwords that are usually accompanied by an influencer on a swing in Bali but there is such power in gratitude and being grateful for what you already have. Each day, just think of three things you are grateful for – they don't have to be big, it can be as simple as an adorable puppy you walked past, a conversation with a friend or how the light hits your pillow in the morning.

Gratitude enhances our sleep quality and makes us happier. It improves relationships, makes us more generous, reduces blood pressure, increases resilience and reduces depressive symptoms by 35%. If that was a pill, you would be popping it, right?

YOUR SELF-CARE RECEIPT	
Early morning walk	$0.00
Free online yoga class	$0.00
A hot bath	$0.00
Meditate with a mask on	$0.00
Bathtime with a book	$0.00
A late-night phone call	$0.00
TOTAL	$0.00

Choose new messages

We believe the messages we tell ourselves, and you can change what the message is. Always be mindful of your inner voice and try to catch yourself from thinking negative thoughts. If we are constantly telling ourselves we are bad with money, our brain will think it and our behaviour will match it.

Instead pick one of the mantras below and repeat it daily to transform your thoughts about money:

- Money flows into my life.
- I will prosper and grow.
- I love money and money loves me.
- Money is my friend.
- I am grateful for everything that I receive.

Reframe

I went for a run at the start of the new year and after 500 metres I was feeling pretty puffed out. Instead of getting annoyed at myself,

I reframed. I said, 'I'm getting fitter,' and then as I was running up the final hill, I kept saying it over and over to myself, 'I'm getting fitter! I'm getting fitter!' By the end, I was practically high-fiving myself! Had I been running up that hill saying, 'You're so unfit, why did you let yourself get so unfit,' I would have started the day feeling really bad about myself and probably wouldn't have even finished the run. It was such a small mindset shift, but it made a big difference.

We can reframe other messages we tell ourselves as well, especially about money.

- I'm bad with money. → I'm getting better with money every day!
- I'll never be able to afford a house. → I'm saving for a house, I'm going to be a homeowner soon.
- Getting out of debt feels impossible. → I have a plan and I'm working on it every day.
- Money is bad. → Money is a tool that will give me freedom and control over my life.
- If I buy that, I'll have nothing left. → There's always more where that came from.

Other things you can do to help rewire your brain

- The 21-day abundance challenge by Deepak Chopra (find it on the resources page on our website).
- Create a vision board with your goals using some magazines and a big canvas. I love doing this with friends (plus they have a better range of magazines).
- Keep $50 in your wallet or pocket to remind you that abundance is all around.
- Test drive your dream car.
- Donate money to a charity you're passionate about, which will help shift your mindset from scarcity to abundance.

That's a wrap!

Thinking about your past and your money mindset will give you a better idea of how and why you manage your money the way you do. It might give you a bit of insight into how your partner or one of your friends thinks about money too. Remember to forgive yourself for past money mistakes, unblock negative money beliefs, choose positive messages to tell yourself about money, learn what actually makes you happy and remind yourself what you're grateful for.

To action with your gal pals

- ☐ Fill out your early money memories.
- ☐ Discuss what money would look like if it came to tea (or cocktails).
- ☐ Answer the questions about your money beliefs.
- ☐ List three of your biggest money blocks.
- ☐ Pick a new mantra each.
- ☐ Reframe your negative messages into positive ones.
- ☐ Create a vision board for your future.

CHAPTER 2

Time to #Adult

When I was first out of uni and working in the corporate world, I always felt like I had to spend every single cent I earned. I mean that's why we make money, right, to spend it?

That might sound weird if you're a saver, but I felt uncomfortable if I had excess money in my bank account at the end of the month.

A year (okay, 2.5 years) after I had landed that job, my mum sat me down to have a 'money talk'. She wanted to know why I was constantly borrowing money from my sister, which I always (usually) paid back. Where was my money going?

I immediately went into panic mode. I got super defensive, I even felt light-headed and started crying (dramatic much?). Where did all this emotion come from? We were just talking about that thing I use every day – money.

At this moment, I could completely connect with Carrie Bradshaw when she said, 'Where did all my money go? … I know I made some.'

PS Carrie, you spent it on shoes.

Note: Keep Carrie as a fashion icon (not a finance icon).

Telling my mum about my spending felt like I was revealing a dirty secret. I was embarrassed that I had no idea where my money was going. I was actually pretty sure a majority of it was either being used on either drinks, brunch or shopping, or a combination of all three, but I thought that's what everyone did.

I was so annoyed with myself when I realised how much I was wasting compared with what I could have saved.

What was stopping me from taking charge of my money? Was it because I didn't want to accept I was now an adult with responsibility? Would I have to start buying my own trainers, cheese and vitamins – the adulting things? Was I ready for this independence? Well, too bad, because it was here.

Become a goal-getter

What helped me get focused in the end was having a goal. I wanted to move to London by myself, and that meant no more sister credit. I also knew if I got super desperate and needed to borrow from my parents it would take a few days for the money to get to my account. I had to get my money shit together – there was no one I could rely on except for myself.

For my London adventure, I made a goal of $8000: $2000 on flights and then $3000 to travel around for a few months (it was a budget hostel kind of holiday), and the rest to set myself up to live, find a job and pay a bond.

I was desperate to move to the UK. And when I started focusing on saving money and being mindful about how much I was spending, something really interesting happened. More money would enter and stay in my life and saving became a lot easier than I thought. I still did fun things – instead of saying no to brunch, I would suggest going for a walk or grabbing a coffee. And none of my friends cared or judged me, they were excited for me and my new adventure!

NICE WAYS OF SAYING IT'S NOT IN MY BUDGET without sounding stingy
'I'd love to hang out, but rather than go out, shall we have a drink on my balcony?'
'Instead of dinner, let's do breakfast!' – dinner is the most $$ of the meals ...
'What about instead of X restaurant, we try Y? I know they have a $2 taco night! YUM!' #Mexcellent
'I haven't budgeted it in for this month – can we do it next month?'
'I know it's been so long since we've seen each other – let's do coffee!'
'Yes, let's do something fun! What about ... [insert a low-cost activity like a walk, tennis, coffee, visiting a gallery, park run, museum ...]'
'I'm just going to buy my own drinks, as I might have to leave early, but you do rounds without me!'

Where to begin

How do we go about sorting out our money situation if everything feels a bit financially messy? First of all we need to look at the bigger picture: just what is your financial situation?

Net worth

Let's start with a simple exercise to work out your net worth – what you're worth on paper. I know you're so much more than some numbers on a page and your self-worth isn't determined by your financial worth, but we need a starting point.

Your personal net worth is the combination of everything you own (assets) minus everything you owe (liabilities). This can be a positive or negative number, and it's a good reflection of where you stand financially at any given time.

If you're a net worth virgin, don't worry – we've got you (the first time I did this I was 32 years old).

Grab a pen and paper (or for my spreadsheet warriors out there you can download our template from the resources page on our website).

List out your assets

An asset is something you own that makes you money.

Assets may include:

- Cash in the bank
- The total amount of your superannuation or pension
- The current value of your car (if fully paid off)
- The current value of your home
- Valuable personal belongings you own outright (laptop, jewellery)
- Any investments you have, such as property, ETFs or shares

2 List out your liabilities

Liabilities are what you owe others. In short, assets put money in your pocket, and liabilities take money out.

For example, if you buy a car on loan and pay monthly interest on the loan, then your vehicle should be considered a liability because it takes money away from you and also decreases in value.

Liabilities may include:

- Credit card debt
- Student debt
- Personal loans
- Mortgage
- Car loan
- Money owed on any Buy Now Pay Laters (BNPL)
- Any money you owe family or friends
- Anything that requires a monthly payment to keep

Robert Kiyosaki, author of *Rich Dad Poor Dad*, says, 'The rich buy assets. The poor only have expenses. The middle class buys liabilities they think are assets.'

I see this all the time when guys buy boats, jet skis or watches – they think they are assets, but they are liabilities because they are going down in value. Ladies, unless that bag is vintage Hermes, it ain't an asset!

What if I have a mortgage?

What's left of the loan is a liability and the current value of your home is an asset. If you don't know the current value of your home then get a valuation, see what houses are going for on realestate.com.au or look at similar properties in your area.

3 Work out your net worth

Now take your liabilities away from your assets to get your net worth (how much you are worth on paper).

Assets – liabilities = net worth

If you do this calculation and it comes out in the red (a negative number), don't freak out. There's always a solution to get out of debt. At least you now have a starting point and we can start working out how to get you back in the black (a positive number).

We want to see our net worth increase over time. It's exciting when you see your money growing and you can be #Grateful for the money flowing into your bank account!

WHAT IS YOUR NET WORTH?	
ASSETS what you own	
Laptop	$
Super fund	$
Cash	$
Investments	$
Car (what it's worth)	$
Property	$
TOTAL =	$
LIABILITIES what you owe	
Student debt	$
Mortgage	$
Car loan	$
Personal loan (Afterpay etc.)	$
Fines or tickets	$
Credit card debt	$
TOTAL =	$
ASSET TOTAL – LIABILITIES TOTAL = NET WORTH	

The dreaded B-word

Now that you know your net worth, it's time to get your budget in order. I can already hear you, '*Nooo, not a budget, that's so boring, it's gonna take me ages. Can't I just do the calculations in my head?*' Think of a budget as just allocating money to different areas of your life and making sure the money goes where you want it to. You might think it means counting every penny and stopping yourself from having fun, but it actually lets you have fun without the guilt that you might be overspending.

To budget properly, you first need to make sure you know how much you are actually earning.

Action 1 Work out how much you are earning

It's time to look at your payslip (yes, they are still a thing). If you're an employee it's most likely this is automatically sent to you via email. (If you can't find it, call HR or payroll and ask them for a copy, or your login to the payroll portal.) If you're self-employed you're going to do some basic maths.

A Ladies Finance Club survey found that only 50% of us check our payslips regularly. Mistakes do happen so check you are being paid correctly.

If your salary is $75,000 a year, that divided by 12 months is not how much is hitting your account each month. We want the number that hits your bank account (also known as the net amount). Lisa Simpson, a beloved LFC Ambassador and financial counsellor, has this great saying: 'Gross is how many fish are in the sea, but if I drop my net into the sea, I can only take home what is in my net.' And that's your net pay, your pay with tax taken out.

GROSS VS NET

Gross is how many fish are in the sea. **(Total pay)**

If I drop my net in the sea I can only take home with me what's in my net.
(Net = tax taken out)

Payslip checklist

The main things we want you to look out for are:

- [ ] That the amount of money your payslip says is hitting your account matches what actually hits your account.
- [ ] That you are being paid your superannuation and that the amount you are being paid is correct (yes, mistakes do happen). The rate increased to 10.5% in 2022 and will increase again in 11% in 2023. More on that in Chapter 7!
- [ ] That the pay rate is what you've agreed to in your position description. If it's lower than what you agreed to speak to your manager; if it is higher than what you agreed to, check with your manager that it's correct. You don't want to have to pay it back! If you're aware of any pay increase, check that you have received it.
- [ ] What, if any, fringe benefits (salary packaging) you are receiving. A fringe benefit is something extra that you get from your employer, in addition to your wage or salary, or in return for forgoing some of your salary under a salary sacrifice arrangement. It normally saves you on tax.
- [ ] Your sick and holiday leave balance – make sure it is correct.
- [ ] That your HECS/HELP student debt (if you have one) is being deducted if you're above the repayment threshold.

If you receive a government payment as income, this information can be found by checking your income statement.

EXAMPLE PAY SLIP

PAY NO: 7994 PAY DATE: 14 AUG 2022 ← Your pay date (day the money hits your account)

PAY PERIOD 29 JUL 2022 TO 11 AUG 2022 ← Pay period (so this person is getting paid fortnightly)

COMPONENT	THIS PAY	YTD **Year to Date** Since the start of the financial year	DATE	HOURS Hours taken	RATE Hourly rate
Annual Lve Annual Leave	0.00	299.60			
Pers Lve Personal Leave (sick leave etc.)	389.85	389.85		9.60 How much personal leave was taken this pay period	40.6094
Normal How many hours you NORMALLY work	2079.24	7880.01		51.20 Worked 51.20 hours this pay period	40.6102 Paid $40.61 per hour
MV Alw 78c Motor vehicle allowance	0.00	67.08			
A/L Loading Annual leave loading	0.00	52.43			
GROSS Without tax taken out	2469.09	8688.97			
TAXABLE Salary liable for taxation	1750.64	5815.17			
TAX Amount you have been taxed	278.00	850.00			
SalPacCTAS Salary sacrifice/packaging/ fringe benefits	718.45	2873.80			
TOTAL DEDN Total deductions	718.45	2873.80			
NET How much goes into your bank account	1472.64	4965.17			
Hesta SGC Super account (9.5%)	234.56	819.07			

LEAVE TAKEN:

TYPE DESCRIPTION	START DATE	END DATE	HOURS TAKEN
PER Personal Leave	08 Aug 2022	08 Aug 2022	7.6000
PER Personal Leave	01 Aug 2022	01 Aug 2022	2.0000

LEAVE ENTITLEMENTS:

Annual Leave Total: 45.19 H

Personal Leave Total: 6.05 H

How much leave you have taken this pay period and how much you have remaining

Jargon schmargon

Salary sacrificing is when you arrange to receive less take-home pay from your employer and in return your employer pays for benefits out of your pre-tax salary. A common benefit might be contributing more super.

For example, you might package a salary of $100,000 so that you receive:

$85,000 as income

$15,000 super as a benefit

This reduces your taxable income to $85,000. You can benefit as you may pay less income tax.

But, Molly, I'm self-employed!

If you run a business, are a sole trader or in a partnership, it's a little bit more work. Look back over the last six months, or preferably 12 months, of your income and calculate the monthly average. Use the lowest figure. It's always better to budget on a lower income and earn more money than to budget on your once-off (potential) income and earn less.

Action 2 Find out how much is going out

Most of us could name the Kardashian sisters but not our own monthly expenses.

We want this budget to be as realistic as possible so we need to know what to base it around. So, before we set new targets, let's look at where your money is currently going.

There are two ways to do this:

Option 1 – Print or download three months' worth of bank statements. You can do this by logging into your bank account, going to your statements and downloading them.

Option 2 – Download a budgeting app. What I love about budgeting apps is that they categorise your spending for you, so you can see your past money behaviours. Also, most banks –including NAB, Commonwealth Bank and UP Bank – have a budget breakdown section as part of your online banking account. Prefer to use an app? Check out WeMoney or Frollo. The government's Moneysmart website also has a web-based app.

For either option, head over to ladiesfinanceclub.com/money and fill out the 'Old You' template tab with this information (you can even estimate how much you think you spend in each category before finding out the real answer).

Budget categories include:

INCOME	GROCERIES	TRANSPORT & AUTO
Your take-home pay	Supermarket	Bus, train & ferry
Your partner's take-home pay	Fruit & veg market	Petrol (or power if you charge your car)
Bonuses and/or overtime	Food subscription box (Marley Spoon, HelloFresh etc.)	Road tolls & parking
Income from savings and investments	Pet food	Rego & licence
Centrelink benefits	Other	Repairs & maintenance
Family benefit payments		Fines
Child support received		Airfares
Other		Other

ENTERTAINMENT & EATING OUT

- Coffees out
- Lunches
- Takeaway
- Drinks & alcohol
- Going out
- Restaurants
- Online subscriptions
- Streaming services (e.g. Netflix)
- Holidays
- Books
- Gifts (Christmas etc.)
- Fun stuff (dance classes, comedy etc.)

HOME & UTILITIES

- Mortgage or rent
- Body corporate fees
- Council rates
- Furniture & appliances
- Renovations & maintenance
- Electricity
- Gas
- Water
- Internet
- Phone

CHILDREN

- Baby products
- Toys
- Babysitting
- Child care
- Sports & activities
- School fees
- Excursions
- School uniforms
- Other school needs
- Child support payment
- Other

INSURANCE & FINANCIAL

- Car insurance
- Home & contents insurance
- Personal & life insurance
- Health insurance
- Car loan
- Credit card interest
- Other loans (e.g. BNPL)
- Paying off debt
- Investments & super contributions
- Pet insurance
- Charity donations
- Other

PERSONAL & MEDICAL

- Cosmetics & toiletries
- Hair & beauty
- Medicines & pharmacy
- Glasses & eyecare
- Dental
- Doctors & medical
- Hobbies
- Clothing & shoes
- Jewellery & accessories
- Computers & gadgets
- Sports & gym
- Education
- Pet care & vet
- Other

SAVINGS GOALS

Remember to include any money you put towards your savings goals as well. Treat them like bills.

A need vs a want

A 'need' is a must-have – something you need to survive, like paying your electricity bill, mortgage or rent.

A 'want' is a nice thing to have – something you can live without, like getting Netflix. (Although during Covid it was debatable whether or not Netflix was actually a 'need'. But you get the gist.)

It's important to ensure that we are always covering our needs first.

Action 3 Create a 'new you' budget

What's happened in the past has happened and there's no point beating yourself up over it or having a pity party for one. It's time to forgive yourself for past spending frenzies and focus on the new you – and a budget for the new you. It's legit exciting!

What matters to you

Take the time to look at your spending and understand what really matters to you. If you need your daily coffee at your local coffee shop for your mental health – then keep it, that's the beauty of the budget. (Whisper voice: it's your budget so you can change the different amounts and balance it out.)

If you're struggling to work out what's actually important to you then put an H (high), M (medium) or L (low) next to each category based on whether these things are a priority for you: daily coffee, car expenses, alcohol, shoes, kitchen gadgets, dry-cleaning, Spotify, Netflix, presents, big nights out, council tax, taxis, computer games, pretty furniture, education and courses, weekend breaks, donating money, insurance, debt repayments, medicine, haircuts, utility bills, rent, clothes, eating out, sport, pet costs.

We have two options for creating the 'new you' budget – it's like pick your own adventure. You can choose *The Zero-based Method* or the *50/30/20 Rule*. No two people are the same so your budget doesn't have to be the same as your gal pals' or partner's.

The Zero-based Method

With the Zero-based Method, we are giving every dollar a job.

When you are using this method to create a new budget in a spreadsheet or app we recommend you follow this order:

1. Input the money you need to save for your goals first; we call this 'paying yourself first'. If we only save what's left after spending – you guessed it – there is rarely anything left to save. You can spend years and years working and have nothing to show for it (*cough*, this could have been me).
2. Make sure you're covering your most basic needs, or as American money guru Rachel Cruze calls them: the four walls of your house, including Shelter (rent, mortgage), Food (groceries), Utilities (bills, debt repayments) and Transport (car costs, fuel).
3. Allocate the rest of your money among the other categories. Look at you – budgeting like a boss!

ZERO-BASED BUDGETING

1. **Write down your monthly income.**
2. **Write down your monthly expenses.**
   Don't forget the priorities first – that's food, utilities, shelter and transportation. Also, remember to put away some money for your goals.
3. **Write down your seasonal expenses.**
   Christmas, birthdays etc.
4. **Subtract your expenses from your income to equal zero.**
   Should = $0. If not, you need to reduce your expenses.
5. **Track your spending throughout the month.**
   It's the only way you'll know if your spending lines up with your plan.

Set up your Zero-based accounts

You know when you have a messy wardrobe and it's hard to see what you own? It's the same for your finances. It's important to have more than one account, otherwise things are just going to get messy quickly.

Imagine trying to save for a house, pay your bills and spend your 'fun money' all from the one account. Instead, set up different fee-free accounts and give them fun labels (you can do this via your online banking).

EXAMPLE ACCOUNTS

ACCOUNT	WHAT IT'S FOR	GIVE IT A NAME
Account 1	Food, Fuel, Fun and Incidentals	(FFFI)
Account 2	Bills and regular payments	(Adulting)
Account 3	Saving goals	(Future Dream Pad or France 2025)
Account 4	Emergencies	(OMG fund)

I'm a big believer that everyone is different, so the beauty of this is you can create as many accounts as you want. Don't overcomplicate it though; I personally wouldn't have more than five.

> Giving your accounts names will help you stop transferring from one to the other – who wants to take money from their Future Dream Pad account? Not me!

The 50/30/20 Rule

If you don't like the Zero-based Method (personal finance is personal so what works for you might not work for your gal pal) you might prefer what we call the 50/30/20 Rule.

This is where you split your money up into different accounts and work off three percentages. It's similar to the Zero-based Method because you set up multiple accounts but different because you aren't accounting for every dollar.

You will need:

- An **Adulting** account: 50% of your pay goes to living expenses (the boring but necessary stuff – your four walls of shelter, food, utilities and transport).
- A **Fun** account: 30% of your pay to spend on fun stuff like entertainment, shopping, dinners out, holidays and beauty.
- A **Future Me** account: 20% of your pay goes to growing your money, whether that be investing or saving for a house.
- An **OMG** account: This is where your emergency fund lives, for things like your car breaking down, losing your job or getting injured. If 2020 hasn't convinced you of the need for this account, nothing will! We have a whole chapter (Chapter 4) on this coming up.

SET YOUR BANK ACCOUNTS UP FOR SUCCESS

INCOME

LIVING EXPENSES

Rent, Mortgage, Food, Bills ...

50% of your pay

FUTURE ME

Investments, Additional Super

20% of your pay

FUN MONEY

Holidays, Brunch, Going Out, Clothes ...

30% of your pay

OMG FUND
(emergency savings)

3–6 months of expenses

Separate bank

The 50/30/20 Rule is just a rule of thumb, so if you're going to use it, it's important to look at your past spending to make sure these percentages work for you. Otherwise you might need to adjust them or reduce your spending.

When I speak to some of our LFC members, they tell me they get into the habit of doing sneaky little transfers from their Adulting account into their Fun account. If this is you, perhaps think about why you're doing this. Are you not connecting with your bigger goals or do you need to break your spending down further? Are you doing it after a few drinks? Work out what the trigger is and put steps in place to stop that behaviour (e.g. removing your card details from your favourite online shops).

Sherri Dumbrell from Essential Spending Planner, who has also run sessions for LFC, says, 'Having a clear purpose for each bank account will prevent you from stealing from one account to pay for something in another account. Stop sabotaging your financial goals by stealing from yourself!'

Automatic payments

Now you have two budgets: your 'old you' budget (with your old spending habits) and your sparkling 'new you' budget (your future budget).

Whether your new budget is the Zero-based Method or the 50/30/20 Rule, it's important to set up automatic payments on your account so you're not having to manually move money (especially if you're a natural spender). We want to remove as much decision-making as possible. You can set up automatic transfers so that the day after you get paid, the money automatically splits out across your different accounts (without you having to do it). Ain't technology great?

I am a spender so I have an automatic transfer set up each Monday morning so I know how much I can spend for the rest of the week.

How do you set up an automatic transfer?

You can set this via your online banking by scheduling transfers from one of your accounts to another. You can choose the amount, how often this happens and even set an end date on it. All banks will have this feature.

Will I be charged?

There are no charges to transfer money between your own accounts within a bank.

What's a direct debit?

A direct debit is an automatic payment that transfers money from your account to another account, like a gym membership or mobile payment. The beauty of setting up direct debits or automatic payments is that you don't have to remember to find logins or pay the bill, and you won't be charged any pesky late fees.

It's important to review your direct debits every few months and always ensure you have enough money in your account. When you want to stop a direct debit, you can just cancel it via your bank or via the providers you set it up with.

One thing to note about direct debiting is that it allows the company to access your bank account to pay your bill. Setting up a regular BPAY or transfer schedule instead allows you to be in control of paying your bills via direct credit because you have the power to cancel it.

Are you making these budgeting mistakes?

When you make your budget make sure you remember to include money for:

- Special occasions such as Christmas, birthdays and anniversaries.
- Things you will need to replace such as washing machines, dishwashers, tyres and car expenses (that's why we will have an emergency fund).
- Holidays.
- Personal care – hair, beauty products (it's expensive being a lady, am I right?).
- Kid-related expenses – extra activities, clothes, extra child care.
- Annual bills such as council rates and car insurance. Write out the due dates and stick them on your fridge to help you remember.
- Invisible spending such as those 'quick' trips to Kmart, Priceline, Target or a cafe, which can be good at messing up your budget.

What if my budget is coming out negative?

You're not the first person that this has ever happened to nor will you be the last, but if it's coming out negative you have two options: spend less or earn more. That's it.

There are lots of practical ways you can spend less.

Negotiate on bills

You should be doing this once a year minimum. If you don't, Joel Gibson, author of *Kill Bills!*, says, 'you could be losing hundreds of dollars a year … You need to be disloyal to the providers of your household bills.'

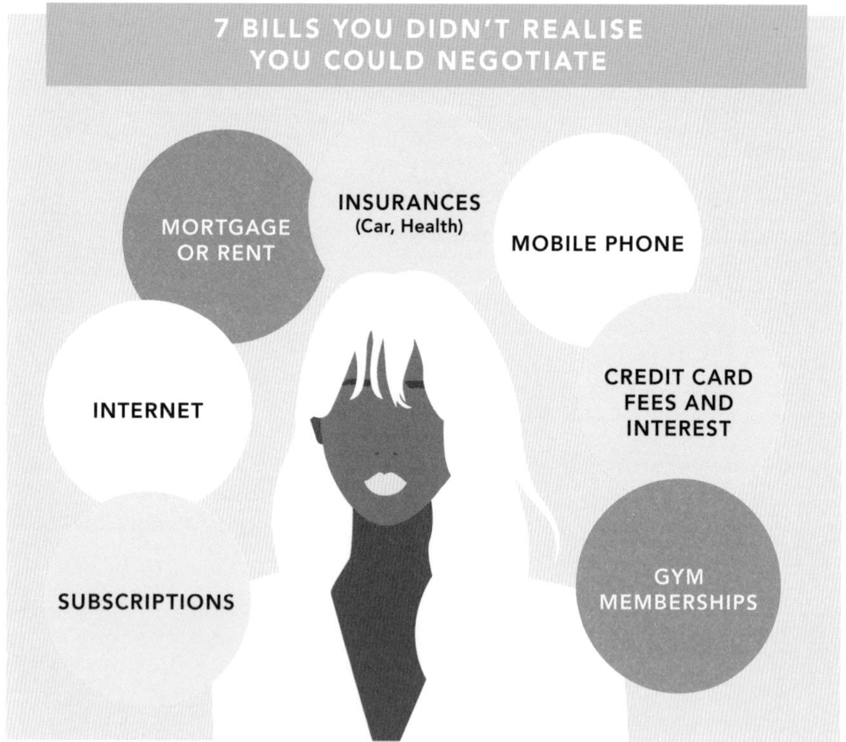

Joel says to 'mystery shop' your providers. Sign up as if you're a new customer (use a different email address) to see what the best price is. If you find you're losing out, give them a ring and see what better deals you can get. (This actually works!)

Cashback sites

The two main sites in Australia are ShopBack and Cashrewards. When you use these websites you get money back on everyday purchases online, like when you buy clothes, insurance, flights or book hotel rooms. I have had hundreds of dollars put back into my cashback account, which I then transfer to my bank account!

Reduce your utility bills

Check out Energy Made Easy – a government comparison site that lets you compare energy prices.

It's also a good idea to get your bill admin sorted – set up a folder on your computer or a folder in your email (since most bills are sent via email) and store all your bills in one place.

Create a meal plan

When people say, 'Oh, I meal prep, it saves me hundreds,' I'm like, 'How? Where do you get the recipe ideas and the timeeeee?' But, seriously, food is our biggest household bill. Australians waste around $2500 a year in edible food so it's worth coming up with a meal plan – we have created some meal plan templates for you on our online resources page (you're welcome)! Some people love going to the store, but if you prefer to spend your time out of grocery stores then do your shopping online – you're more likely to stick to your list and less likely to impulse purchase. Woolies and Coles let you pick recipes out online and then add the contents straight to your cart. Love a time hack!

I was talking to a single friend who works full time and she said the last thing she wants to do after a long day is cook dinner. Instead, she began ordering fresh meals to her door, from companies like Youfoodz and Soulara. Although it's a little more expensive, it saves her more money than if she were making dinner at home, especially if she adds up the wasted food (plus her time of buying it and cooking it). One dinner costs her anywhere from $11 to $15 and she likes that it provides portion control and the meals are healthy, 'Plus I don't have to do any washing up and it all comes in recyclable containers'.

If you also find it hard to find the brain space to decide what to cook every night you might want to look at DIY options like Marley Spoon and HelloFresh where all the ingredients and recipes are delivered to you and you just need to put it together.

Be a savvy shopper

Thanks to consumer groups all supermarkets have to display how much you are paying per unit, so make sure you're getting bang for your buck!

When you're in the grocery store also be sure to look up and down the shelf. Some brands pay for their location in the supermarket – the most expensive brands are usually at eye level and are at the start and end of the aisles.

Most of the supermarkets put out their specials on a Wednesday. Finally, don't go shopping hungry – this is a very important one for me as I always seem to be hungry.

Reduce your fuel bill

There are multiple fuel apps, such as Petrol Spy or Fuel Map Australia, that will show you the cheapest fuel in your area. The NSW government even runs fuelcheck.nsw.gov.au. I have seen price differences of 50 cents between petrol stations a kilometre down the road from each other.

Ask yourself: 'Do I really need this?'

When shopping in real life (yes, it's still a thing) or online, look at this checklist before you pay, and wait 24 hours if you're unsure! Our homes are full of 'stuff'. Landfill is full of 'stuff'. You're now a money-savvy lady, so think mindfully, channel your inner Marie Kondo and think, 'Will this bring me joy?'

These savings won't make you a millionaire overnight but the small amounts compound over time! As my mother (and thousands of others) says, 'Watch the pennies and the pounds follow.'

CHECKLIST BEFORE SPENDING

- ✓ **Do I have something similar at home?**
- ✓ **I exchange my time and energy for money – is this worth it?**
- ✓ **Do I need this now or can it wait?**
- ✓ **How many hours does it cost me?**
- ✓ **Is this an emotional decision?**
- ✓ **Did I intend to buy this?**

Here are some budgets of some of our members

LFC MEMBER 1: Single, early 40s, no kids

Job: Nanny and freelance event florist as a side hustle

Income per month: $4500 net + $30 from investments

Home + utilities: $2009

Insurances + financials: $287

Groceries: $240 ($60/week average)

Personal + medical: $300

Entertainment + eating out: $280

Transport + auto: $316

Children: N/A

$1098 surplus per month

LFC MEMBER 2: Couple, early 30s, two kids
Job: Tradie (him) / maternity leave (her)
Income per month: $8200 net, no investments
Home + utilities: $2000
Insurances + financials: $600
Groceries: $1800
Personal + medical: $1600
Entertainment + eating out: $650
Transport + auto: $900
Children: $550
$100 surplus per month

LFC MEMBER 3: Couple, late 30s, three kids
Job: Architect (him) / student and homemaker (her)
Income per month: $13,750 net, no investments
Home + utilities: $2800
Insurances + financials: $700
Groceries: $2300
Personal + medical: $3300
Entertainment + eating out: $2400
Transport + auto: $1100
Children: $1400
$250 deficit per month

How do I get my partner on board?

If you're a saver and your partner is a spender, you're not destined to fail. You just need to be clear on your money goals together and explain that a budget doesn't limit their spontaneity but it gives you both freedom and permission to spend. It's also important that you each have your own 'fun money' you can spend without each other's permission.

That's a wrap!

You don't need a complicated spreadsheet to get on top of your money: you just need to be clear about your priorities and goals. If your life is seriously busy right now, and you can only do one thing, then automate your saving goals and pay yourself first! You don't want to get to the end of the working year and realise you haven't actually saved anything for you and your dreams. The key is to remove as much decision-making as possible.

To action with your gal pals

- ☐ Open any new accounts and label them (make sure they are fee-free).
- ☐ Fill out the 'old you' and 'new you' spreadsheets.
- ☐ Pay yourself first – set up an automatic payment for the day after you get paid.
- ☐ Check that your gal pal actually did the budget.
- ☐ On seeing proof that you have both done a budget, clink glasses because you just smashed it!

CHAPTER 3

Go-Getter

There's a quote from *Alice in Wonderland* that my mentor Dale Beaumont shared with me.

> Alice: Would you tell me, please, which way I ought to go from here?
>
> The Cheshire Cat: That depends a good deal on where you want to get to.
>
> Alice: I don't much care where.
>
> The Cheshire Cat: Then it doesn't much matter which way you go.

When I heard this for the first time, it was a bit of a lightbulb moment for me. It is really hard to achieve a goal if you don't know what you want.

Imagine playing a game of netball with no goals – you would just be throwing around a ball. What's the point?

How do you prioritise and stay motivated if you have no direction?

So many of us don't decide what we want to do with our money, we just 'go with the flow' and get caught up in what's happening. 'Oh, the new iPhone is out, I'd better upgrade.' 'Woo, cheap flights, let's go to Bali.' As a result, we can feel financially out of control. This feeling can generally be avoided by making conscious decisions earlier that align with what you really want to get out of life!

Imagine jumping in the car to go to 42 Wallaby Way, Sydney, but just putting Sydney into Google Maps. You'd end up close to your destination, but still might be 100 kilometres away (and you'd never be reunited with Nemo).

When you look at Google Maps you're looking at the next turn, the next roundabout – it's not until you zoom out that you see the bigger picture and what direction you're really going in.

Thanks for coming to my TED Talk. Let's get goal-getting!

Why do some goals fail?

You want to reach your goals so let's make sure you don't make the most common goal-setting mistakes.

1 We make our goals too big

Business and executive coach Dr Laura Hills coined the phrase 'Goldilocks Goals' to describe goals that are not too soft, not too hard, but 'just right'. For example, saying, 'I'm never going to order Uber Eats again,' when you currently order five times a week might be a tad unrealistic, although reducing it to once a week might be achievable. Or saying, 'I want to buy a million-dollar beachfront house next year,' when your salary is $75,000 a year might not be super realistic. Don't get me wrong, I am all for aiming high and pushing yourself out of your comfort zone but if your goals are too big you might give up before you start.

Aussie entrepreneur Courtney Mangan says, 'Remember you don't want to feel bullied by your goals, they are there to motivate you.'

2 Our goals are too vague

One of the most common New Year's resolutions I hear is 'I want to save money'. To which I always respond, 'How much? What for? By when? Why?' Generally, I'm met with a blank expression. Without trying to get all corporate wank speak on you, it's important that we make our goals SMTAR. Specific, Measurable, Time-bound, Attainable, Relevant. (Yes, call me cray cray, I have mixed the SMART goals up – read on to find out why!)

Specific

Get as detailed as you can about what you want to achieve. Close your eyes and see it!

Not specific: I want to buy a house.

Specific: I want to buy a three-bedroom house on the Gold Coast within 15 minutes of the beach.

Measurable

As the saying goes, 'what gets measured gets improved'. How are you going to measure your goal? It might be dollar amounts, kilometres, a certain level or qualification.

Not measurable: I need to save for a deposit.

Measurable: The average house price where I want to buy is $1 million so I will need to save a deposit of $100,000 (a 10% deposit with Lenders Mortgage Insurance – more on that later).

Time-bound

This is why I have gone all wild on the SMART goal and put the T for Time-bound first – it's hard to work out if a goal is achievable if we don't have a date by when we want to achieve it. This is where breaking a goal down will help you discover if it's realistic.

Not time-bound: Soon.

Time-bound: 1 June 2025.

My personal trainer in the UK gave me exercises with time limits, for example, 'Molly, summer bodies are built in winter, we are planking for two mins.' I would slowly get into my plank position and watch the clock move at a snail's pace for 120 seconds. But, because I had a set time limit, I was motivated to push myself. Had he said, 'We are just going to see how long you can go for,' I definitely would have given up 30 seconds in.

So your goal becomes: I want to buy a three-bedroom house on the Gold Coast within 15 minutes of the beach with a deposit of $100,000, by 1 June 2025 (for example purposes only).

Achievable

This is the time to give yourself a reality check. Is this goal really achievable and realistic considering your circumstances?

If you want to save $100,000 in two years but when you break that down, you don't have enough income to save and pay your bills, you might need to give yourself a longer time frame or find extra ways of making more income.

I'm not saying don't dream big but a goal without a plan is just a wish.

Not achievable: Can't afford to put away $750 per week (for example purposes only).

Achievable: Can afford to put away $250 each month and will find side hustle like taking on another job, getting a pay rise or flipping furniture to bring in the extra income.

Relevant

Here's where you need to think about the big picture. Why are you setting the goal that you're setting? Your goals should align with your values and larger long-term goals. Ask yourself, why is this goal important to me?

Not relevant: My parents want me to buy a house.

Relevant: I want a house to start growing my property empire so I can become financially free. Yipee!

3 They aren't our goals

Who has had a goal that was actually someone else's goal? Maybe your parents' or partner's? Perhaps it's your sibling's and, without realising it, you're competing to be the first one to buy a luxury car, or maybe it is just pressure you feel from society? Recently one of our LFC members, Liz, said, 'I feel like I should buy a property because that's what all my friends are doing and my parents keep pushing me into it, but I really want to travel and live overseas and have no idea where I want to end up.'

If it's not a goal that you truly connect to then you're going to find it really hard to stick to and be motivated to achieve.

This is why we really need to know our 'why' – why we want to achieve that goal. Maybe you want to build an emergency fund so you'll never be trapped in a job or, like our member Cecile, you know you have money to fly back to Germany if anything happens to your family. Writing down your why will keep you motivated.

4 We give up too early

James Clear, author of *Atomic Habits*, says, 'We often dismiss small changes because they don't seem to matter very much in the moment. If you save a little money now, you're still not a millionaire.' We don't see results quickly and we give up and slide back into those old habits.

When we feel like we're making no progress we give up.

If you run every day for two weeks, you're probably not going to be able to do a half marathon, but if you run every day for three months you'll see results.

Investing $50 every week isn't going to feel like much, but consistently doing it over 20 years at 8% return may lead to $100,000.

5 We have no system in place

To achieve good results, you need good systems. For example, automating your savings is a system you have created to help you reach your goals. Likewise, booking in your gym classes every Sunday night into your calendar and making sure you have your gym gear in your bag is a system to support your fitness goal, so make sure you set up your systems!

Let's become goal-getters

It's really hard to save money if you're not saving for something in particular. How will you know when you have enough, or when you have succeeded?

When you have clear money goals it is easier to be disciplined with yourself, because you're saying no to things now so you can say yes to something you really want later!

We often set KPI (key performance indicators) for our work or business, so it's time we set some for ourselves. Thinking about what you want to achieve can be overwhelming – there are millions of things to choose from – so we are going to help you through it.

Grab a piece of paper or pop on over to to our website ladiesfinanceclub.com/money and download our goal-setting template.

Reflect on last year's goals

Ask yourself and your gal pal – what were your goals last year? (Did you even have any?) Did you achieve them or make progress towards them?

What was your most successful moment last year? What was your biggest lesson? What could you improve? What worked well and why? How do you feel about last year as a whole?

What's your time frame?

To make this goal-setting process a little less overwhelming we are going to break our goals into three sections:

- Short (1–3 years)
- Medium (4–6 years)
- Long (8 years plus)

Goal inspiration

It's helpful to read other people's goals as it can inspire us to build and borrow from each other. Here are some from our LFC members:

Short

- Build an emergency fund of $1000
- Get out of $25,000 credit card debt
- Pay off $2500 Afterpay debt
- Build a baby fund of $10,000
- Save for a holiday to New York
- Sort out taxes

Medium

- Save a deposit and buy a house
- Pay for IVF
- Start a side hustle
- Open a bar
- Do a wine course in France

Long

- Take a year off work
- Volunteer for a year in Africa
- Take the family on a cruise
- Buy an investment property
- Retire with a million dollars

If you're not clear on your goals just keep thinking. Think about how much money you want to make and save. How much do you want to invest; do you need to get out of debt, or pay down your mortgage; what fun things do you want to save for?

Many years ago someone asked me what I would do if money wasn't an issue, and I looked blankly at them and said, 'Go to a day spa'. I had no idea. But when I thought about it I realised I'd like to travel to 50 countries, set up charity projects that helped women around the world, go horseback riding in Iceland, create a TV series ... The point being, I had a lot of ideas! I just had to sit back and think. Like a good cuppa, let your ideas brew! There's no rush.

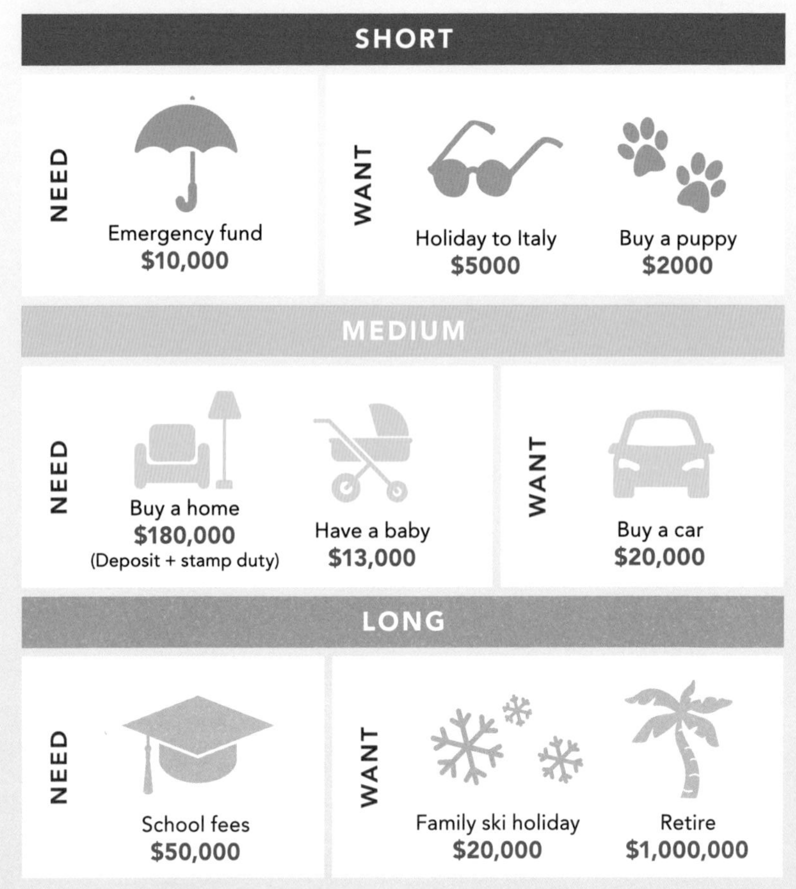

Write your goals down

1. Write your goals down – the wild, the big, the small, the tiny, the silly, the fun. Force yourself to write down at least 20, even if you think they're crazy or ridiculous.
2. Pick three financial goals that you want to make happen this year no matter what and write them as a SMTAR goal.

Do I really have to write down my goals?

You bet you do!

A research study done by psychology professor Dr Gail Matthews found that you're 42% more likely to achieve your goals if you write them down on a regular basis. I like those odds! #Boom

New York Times bestselling author of *Hard Goals* Mark Murphy says, 'People who very vividly describe or picture their goals are anywhere from 1.2 to 1.4 times more likely to successfully accomplish their goals than people who don't.' So get creative in that gorgeous head of yours.

Stick your goals everywhere

Put your goals everywhere so you are reminded of them every day. Please don't put them in a book not to be looked at for another year. Briony Benjamin, bestselling author of *Life Is Tough (But So Are You)* (also my big sis), says, 'Put a copy of your goals on your desktop, phone, your room, work desk, even change your password on your computer,' so you're typing it every day (obvs with some capital letters and symbols for security – House!2025*).

We want to prime our brain to look for ways to achieve that goal. If your goal is to work in Paris for a year at a fashion marketing firm (*cough*, familiar) then you'll find ways to make it happen. You might start noticing

French restaurants, flight sales to France, croissants and French accents popping up everywhere.

Break your goals down

A big goal can seem overwhelming, so it helps to break it down into smaller chunks so you can see your progress and celebrate milestones. Remember, baby steps in the right direction are still steps.

Here's an example:

Goal: Save $10,000 into my emergency fund by December so I can be financially independent from my parents.

1. Open a separate fee-free bank account and label it 'OMG Fund'.
2. Work out a weekly or monthly amount to save into the fund.
3. Set up automatic payments so on payday the money leaves my account and goes into my OMG account.
4. Check in each quarter on my progress.
5. Celebrate! You did it... (also don't forget to stop automatic payments).

Schedule it

You're a money-savvy superstar so you're going to schedule each step you need to take to achieve your goal into your diary or calendar. This will help you work on them every day.

It might take you some time to write out all the steps but stick with it. This is your life and you're in the driver's seat (a scary thought if you knew how I drive).

That's a wrap!

Be daring and be brave with your goals. Not to sound too depresso but if you're 20 years old you've got (on average) around 65 years left; if you're 40 you have 45 years. So make sure your goals are something that are really worth your energy and time – something you're passionate about!

Super successful people like Oprah, Marie Forleo and Spanx founder Sara Blakely all set goals – and now you do too!

Just taking time to really think about what you want to achieve means you're not going to wake up with regret, or be like Alice and just take whatever path. Instead, you've got a plan.

I promise that writing out a goal, making a plan and working on it every day will change your life – don't believe me? Give it a go (wink face).

To action with your gal pals

- ☐ Write out your goals together.
- ☐ Share your top three goals and the next steps you need to take.
- ☐ Schedule your goals into your calendar.
- ☐ Make a special time to catch up to talk about how your goals are tracking (and, yes, they are allowed to change).
- ☐ Clink those glasses or mugs! You're awesome!

CHAPTER 4

Why You Need an OMG Fund

Pour that mimosa ladies because shit is about to get real! Okay, that sounded a little intense but this next step is going to help set you up for a strong financial future.

Be warned, this is the simplest yet hardest chapter. If you can nail this, the rest will be breezy. This is because, as we learnt in Chapter 1, we are creating a new way of thinking. In the words of Pantene, 'It won't happen overnight but follow these Ladies Finance Club steps and it will happen.' (Okay, maybe not a direct quote.)

If Covid taught us anything, it's that random shit that you would NEVER expect to happen happens and we need to be prepared for when it does. During Covid many people were caught out, as they had been busy living the good life, not giving a minute's thought to their finances. Then when they lost their jobs, or their work hours were dramatically reduced, they realised they couldn't cover their expenses anymore because they had been living beyond their means – spending more than they earned.

Life happens

Look, fingers crossed there aren't going to be any more global pandemics (although my Greek alphabet is really coming on), but things like blowing a tyre, cracking a tooth, replacing a fridge, being made redundant, accidentally getting pregnant, becoming single at 50 – these things can happen. Hopefully not all of them, but generally it's a matter of when, not if. I want to make sure that you and your gal pals are prepared!

Financial counsellor Lisa Simpson says so many people she speaks to tell her that once they have an OMG fund saved, they feel like they have fewer emergencies, because when something occurs, they are secure in knowing they can cover it, and they don't need to panic.

One of our LFC members, Sue, knows all too well about this. She was in credit card debt and had been through a separation that had set her back years financially. She learnt to build her OMG fund, which meant when she was given the worst news a mother could get – that her daughter had been diagnosed with blood cancer – she could throw money at the problem. Fifteen months later Sue's daughter was in remission, and Sue had bought her first investment property! I cried when she told me that – I was so proud of how far she had come.

Side note: I find as I get older that lots of things make me cry, especially TikToks of rescue dogs – the humanity!

WTF is an OMG fund?

An OMG fund is my nifty li'l name for an emergency fund, also referred to as a 'rainy day fund', 'sinking fund', or as my mate and financial wellness coach Betsy Westcott calls them, 'an eff-off fund' – 'because you can tell things like bad jobs, bad relationships and bad living situations to eff off'.

Quite simply, it's money you keep in a separate bank account that is only used for an emergency. This is your new safety net. (And the money should be cash in the bank, not money invested into shares, a term deposit, property, and definitely not crypto.)

I know after a few cheeky G and Ts it can be quite hard to tell what is an actual OMG moment or not so here's a list.

NOT AN OMG MOMENT:

- Mister Zimi is on sale!
- Christmas. (Ladies, it comes once every year, this should not be a surprise.)
- Your car registration is due.
- Your partner's birthday or your anniversary (personally something I haven't had to worry about for a while #AllTheSingleLadies).
- It's my sister's birthday and she wants AirPods (real-life example for my sister reading this, hint hint).
- I spent my rent money on flights to Hamilton Island.
- I love drinkies – drinkies for me, drinkies for the randoms at the bar (why am I so generous after two espresso martinis #SuchAGiver 😂).

ACTUAL OMG MOMENT:

- Illness, whether it be yourself or a loved one, and you need to take time off work.
- Unexpected redundancy or job loss.
- You hate your job, your boss is a psychopath, HR is useless and your workplace is more toxic than my hair dye, and you need out asap (no job is worth your health).
- You're unhappy in your relationship and want to leave.
- Natural disaster (flood or fire) impacts your business.
- Accidently tripping on your own foot and having to get taxis everywhere for a month.
- There is a global pandemic.

On a more serious note (and I don't like to get serious often) having an emergency fund means you're never trapped in a situation because of money. Instead you always have control over the situation – whether that be a job that makes you deeply unhappy or a relationship that has turned controlling, or even little things like knowing you can get a taxi when you feel unsafe at night. In my case, when my sister was going through chemo I was able to take two months off work, fly back to Australia and cover my rent and expenses with the money in my OMG fund. If I didn't have that money available, it would have made a very stressful situation so much worse.

Without sounding too dramatic, the first time I saved $1000 it changed my life. I went from feeling like I was always scrambling for money to feeling calmer. I knew if I really, really needed it, I had money sitting there. And in a hectic ever-changing world who wouldn't love a bit more calm in their life?

How to build your OMG fund

I've got three simple steps.

Drumroll, please.

Step 1 Open a fee-free account with a bank separate from your everyday bank

Pop online and open a savings account and name it 'My OMG Fund' or 'Can't Touch This' (or something equally cool). If the bank offers you a card, decline it; if they send it anyway, hide it or cut it up. We want to keep our greasy little mitts off it and don't want to 'accidentally' confuse it with our *fun* spending card – see, I'm on to you. The idea is that this fund is hard to access (but not too hard for an actual emergency).

How do I find a good savings account?

There aren't many high interest savings accounts going around at the moment so focus on fee-free accounts – most banks have this option. But don't let this hold you up, just pick one.

Is my money safe in a bank?

Deposits up to $250,000 in savings accounts and term deposits with Australian banks are protected by the government, so if something were to happen to the bank (which is unlikely), your deposit would be safe. This is part of the Australian Government Financial Claims Scheme.

What's the diff between a savings account and a transaction account?

A savings account earns and pays you interest based on your overall balance (providing certain terms are met). A transaction account is an account that you use on a day-to-day basis into which your wage and other payments can be paid.

Step 2 Deposit $1000 into your OMG account

'Waaaaait, Molly!' (Angry face.) 'Where the fork am I going to pull a thousand big ones from?' If you don't have $1000 already sitting there you're not alone, ME Bank found that a quarter of Aussie households don't either. But you can start small. If you're not a natural saver, no worries, I wasn't either but you can become one. Set yourself a goal of when you want to have the account filled and then work backwards. How do you eat an elephant? One bite at a time. Actually screw elephants, how do you drink a bottle of prosecco? One sip at a time.

Remember you're not just saving $1000, you're also changing your behaviour.

WRITE THIS OUT AND STICK IT SOMEWHERE YOU WILL SEE IT EVERY DAY:

I will have $1000 by (date)	I need to put away	because
	(X amount per payslip)	

The why is important because it will keep you motivated when you're tossing up whether to spend that extra $40 on bottomless sushi or put that money into your emergency fund.

Example: Why I want to save is because it means I don't have to rely on my partner/parent/winning the lotto, and because I know I am on my path to becoming financially secure.

Insert your own version!

Bit of help here, Molly, how do I save $1000?

I spoke with financial planner and founder of SugarMamma.TV, Canna Campbell, who runs the $1000 Project, a fun financial challenge she created to help people shift their money behaviour.

The $1000 Project is about creating extra money in your life. Look at your budget and see what you can cut out. Are there any side hustles you can do, or anything you could sell? The moment you create that extra money, put it into a separate dedicated savings account. When it hits $1000, transfer that money to one of your financial goals – in this case, your OMG account. To learn more, check out Canna's book *The $1000 Project*!

Some ideas to fill your OMG account:

1. Set up a direct debt so on payday some money automatically leaves your account and goes directly into your OMG fund. Boom! You didn't even get a chance to spend it. If you try to do this manually you might find that once you have paid your bills, gone for lunch, bought some new undies, bought a ski suit from Aldi – there is no money left to put in your OMG fund!
2. Reduce your expenses (negotiate those bills) and put that money into your OMG fund.
3. Sell some extra stuff that you don't need. For example, I sold a designer pair of shoes my ex-boyfriend had bought me, a wallet I had never used, and some weights a friend had given me when she moved back to the UK. Cha-ching (someone's trash is another person's treasure). I sold them on Facebook Marketplace but if you have good brands you can also use sites like Etsy (good for vintage items), Depop and the classic eBay. If you have nothing to sell, ask your friends or family for unused items.
4. Does anyone owe you money? Or can you think of any money that you have not claimed yet? Gift cards, tax returns, a cheque Aunt Mildred sent you, the money you lent a friend, dividends, an overdue invoice etc.
5. Participate in paid research or focus groups.
6. Do an extra shift if that's an option in your line of work, or freelance online on Upwork or Fiverr.
7. Use your work bonus.
8. If your birthday is coming up ask for cash (say you're doing the whole minimalist thing and do not need more stuff in your life).
9. Got a small social media following? Promote a product you love through sites such as theright.fit and Tribe.
10. Pot up any plants you can to resell.

11. Offer to babysit, dog walk, wash cars in your local street or deliver food. Remember this is short-term pain for long-term gain; it might not be glamorous, we just need that $1000.

There's a reason I am not saying 'ask for a pay rise', as you'll see when we cover that in Chapter 13 – it should be part of a bigger strategy, not just because you need some extra cash fast!

What if I am in debt? Do I still save $1000?

Always make minimal repayments on your debts (we don't want you getting any more late fees). The finance gurus we work with at LFC also agree that it's better to build your OMG fund with $1000 while paying down debt. If any other emergencies pop up (say your fridge dies) and you don't have $350 to get it fixed, you're likely to just put it on your credit card, getting yourself into more debt.

Can't I just use my credit card for emergencies?

Ladies, as we say at LFC, 'When things get drastic don't stick it on the plastic!'

A credit card is not an OMG fund. Lisa Simpson says she counsels people all the time who got a credit card 'just for an emergency', then all of a sudden they have racked up $10,000 of debt within a few months. 'That's not an emergency fund, that's spending more than you earn.' #LisaTruthBombs

Another client of Lisa's had a credit card excess of $20,000 'in case of an emergency' to which Lisa rightfully replied, 'What kind of emergency is going to cost $20,000?' I mean, the emergency might be in the Bahamas, and you have to fly first class?

We are setting you up with good financial behaviours, and relying on credit cards (borrowing someone else's money) to get you out of a sticky situation is not part of that.

Is $1000 enough?

We want you to build up to $1000 first. In Chapter 6 we will help you work out the total amount you'll need in your OMG fund.

Should I just invest this money into something low risk?

With all investments there is some level of risk, so your OMG fund is money that shouldn't be invested.

Can my partner and I share an OMG fund?

The OMG fund should be in your name only. It's *your* safety net. If anything were to happen to your partner (they suddenly pass away or get in trouble with the law), your joint financial assets (including bank accounts) may automatically be frozen. This can cause difficulties if direct debits for rent or mortgage payments come out of the account in the name of your partner. Or if you want to leave the relationship and they empty the joint account or block you from accessing it – at least with an OMG fund you have access to money and can seek advice.

What if my partner controls the money?

If you don't feel comfortable having a conversation about money with your partner or you're worried about their reaction, we suggest you seek the professional help of a counsellor. If your partner controls all the money because you haven't shown an interest and haven't wanted to get involved, then use this as an opportunity to start learning. You could say that you're reading this totally awesome book (wink) and want to be involved in understanding what your money goals are (how much you'll need for retirement, what investments you have). If it's because they don't 'trust' you managing the money, then seek free financial counselling from Moneycare or Good Shepherd. Just FYI, having opposite spending habits in couples is common (as they say, opposites attract). Chapter 11 is all about talking to your honey about the money.

Should I keep my OMG fund a secret?

Most financial gurus will tell you not to keep secrets but most published financial gurus are men. If a relationship in the past went toxic you might see having some money aside as a necessity. It's your call.

Step 3 Celebrate!

You did it! You have $1000 in your OMG fund and you're no longer one of the one in three Aussies who can't come up with $500 in an emergency. You're getting your money shit together and you deserve to celebrate! I'm thinking spicy margaritas (or virgin margaritas)!

That's a wrap!

For some of you building an OMG fund of $1000 will be easy – you might already have $1000 just sitting there. For others this will be the most you have ever saved and it might take you some time to get there.

For me, setting up my first OMG fund was huge. I had never saved this amount of money before and not spent it! So when I say, 'Just save $1000,' I get that it's not that simple! For some of us, it requires a complete change in our behaviour. We have to break that spending pattern.

We haven't had a pep talk in a while so huddle in. The only person you should be trying to compare yourself to is who you were yesterday, a year ago, five years ago. Personal finance is personal, it's different for everyone. We are all on different journeys and whether it took you five years to get here, 10 or 30 years, you're here now and you're ready to take action. Your friends might find it really easy to save $1000, but they might have started their journey a lot earlier or might have been given a lift straight to the end, while you had to grind and hustle for that first $1000. Remember your money gal pals are there to support and cheer you on, and vice versa – it's not a competition. As Sensei Ogui, Buddhist minister, says, 'A flower does not think of competing with the flower next to it. It just blooms.' Yes, I'm calling you a flower and it's your time to financially bloom!

To action with your gal pals

With your gal pals, write out:

- ☐ What bank you're opening your OMG Fund (savings account) up with and by when (it might take a few days depending on the bank).

  ____

- ☐ When you want to have saved up your $1000 by.

  ____

- ☐ How much you need to put away each week/month to hit that $1000 amount.

  ____

- ☐ Your biggest why around why you want to save this.

  ____

- ☐ How you will feel once you have an OMG fund set up.

  ____

- ☐ Five different ways you could save or make $1000.

  ____

CHAPTER 5

Debt Me Out of Here

Debt sucks (sorry, it's a hard one to sugarcoat). It can be super stressful and constantly play on your mind, from the moment you wake to the time you go to bed.

There might be a number of reasons why you owe money. It might have been because of a loss of income, illness, you are spending more than you earn, or a relationship breakup. You might feel angry with yourself, ashamed or fearful. We hear you – these are all very normal feelings to have. But we need to forgive ourselves for our past mistakes, let go of the anger and give ourselves a plan for getting out of debt. There's always a way.

When it comes to getting out of debt, you've got to really believe you can get out of it yourself, otherwise it's not going to work.

Grab a pen and paper, put a timer on for 15 minutes and write what your life will be like once you're debt-free. If the words don't flow, just keep going until that alarm dings.

Now, let's do this!

(If you're not in debt, take a read anyway as you might be able to help a friend and also avoid getting into any future bad debt.)

Good debt vs bad debt

In *The Wizard of Oz* there is a good witch who we like and a bad witch who is scary, but they are both witches. With debt, there's good debt and bad debt too.

Good debt is credit that makes you richer using someone else's money (yippee!). For example, a mortgage where the asset (property) you have borrowed against has the ability to increase in value.

A bad debt is money you have borrowed that has a high interest rate, and often decreases in value. This is also known as consumer debt.

Lisa Simpson says, 'It's really important to know that if your name is on it – you own it, and you own the debt. If your name is on the loan, a utility bill, a rent agreement, or even a car loan, then you have to pay 100% of the payment, regardless of what the other party is doing.'

If Jack and Jill go to Harvey Norman and buy $5000 worth of furniture '18 months interest-free', then Jack buggers off up the hill, never to be seen again, poor Jill still has to pay 100% of the debt.

Don't catch an STD (sexually transmitted debt)

Unfortunately, women can fall victim to this and find that their names have been used on loans for which they receive no benefit, such as a partner who has taken out a car loan in their name, but the woman has never driven the car. If your name is on the loan and your partner bails with the car, you are unfortunately liable for the debt. This can have a massive effect on your financial future and future borrowing capacity. If you find yourself in this situation, reach out and get help. We have listed some places you can contact at the end of the book. But, ladies, repeat after me, 'I will not sign anything I don't understand.'

Snowball vs the avalanche

There are two tried and tested methods for getting out of debt, and you may prefer one or the other depending on how your brain works.

For either method, you need to write down all your bad debts on a piece of paper or Excel spready. List them all out – the big, the small, the ugly, the terrifying. The car loans, credit cards, the Afterpays, the Zip pays, #AllThePays, the money you owe your sister, store cards, parking tickets, speeding tickets, rental arrears, laybys – all the debts!

Avalanche method

This is where you're tackling the debt with the highest interest rate first.

1. Write out all your debts and list them in order from the debt with the highest interest rate to the one with the lowest interest rate.
2. Make the minimum repayments on all your debts. If you're able to, set up an automatic transfer on any credit cards so your minimum balance is always paid and you'll never be hit with a late fee.
3. Use any extra funds to pay off the debt with the highest interest rate. This might be a credit card with a 20% interest rate.

Some people like the avalanche method because it makes financial sense to them. But if you have really massive debt and you're hacking away at it, it's really tempting to give up because you're not going to see the results for a while.

Snowball method

This is the most popular among LFC members. It's also the proven method made famous by well-known financial guru and author Dave Ramsey, and which the Barefoot Investor, Scott Pape, also agrees with.

1. List out your debts from the smallest amount you owe to the largest, as well as the minimum monthly repayment. (It's really important that you continue to pay the minimum monthly repayment on each debt.)

For those with a credit card, you need to get drastic and ditch the plastic. You need to stop spending, and this can be the hardest part, especially if you're trapped in a debt cycle. We need to get rid of the card (the source of the pain) so it's time to do some plastic surgery: cut it up, melt it, cancel it, freeze it in a bowl of water – whatever works for you.

Credit card negotiations

This is a really good opportunity for you to call your creditors and ask them for a reduced interest rate, rather than using a balance transfer or consolidating the loans into one. A balance transfer is when you move the amount you owe (the balance) to another credit card (usually with a 0% interest rate for a period of time). *Financial Times* money mentor Lindsay Cook says a balance transfer is like moving the deckchairs around on the Titanic – you're just delaying the inevitable. Instead, research your competitors and use the competing credit card offers as a way to negotiate. Ask them what's the best rate they can offer you. If they still say no, ask them to waive the annual fee. The worst they can say is no.

2. Start paying as much as possible off the smallest debt first. You want to focus any spare cash you get and smash the smallest debt until it's done! Once you have done that you're now officially on a roll to becoming debt-free, baby!
3. After the first debt is paid off, aim and fire again at the second debt. Roll the minimum monthly repayment you were making on that first debt onto the second debt and then pay as much as possible off it.

This technique works because when you pay off your first debt, you have a sense of achievement, your brain gets that hit of dopamine and it builds momentum to keep going. But when you pay a little bit off a big debt (the avalanche method) it's harder to see the progress and you can lose motivation. Remember to celebrate the small wins (just nothing too grand, I'm thinking a cupcake and iced latte, not an overseas trip) then use the momentum to keep going (like a snowball)!

What's the go with student debt?

HECS, or HELP as it was rebranded, is the Australian loan you get through uni to pay for your education. It stands for Higher Education Loan Program (use that for your next trivia night). You'll probably know if you have one, but if you haven't seen it for a while pop on to myGov and check what your balance is.

Once you earn above a certain amount, part of your wage will automatically start being deducted. And, yes, even if you move overseas you still have to pay it.

If you're an employee, some of your pay will be withheld by your employer to cover your repayments. If you're self-employed, you pay once you've filed your tax return – so you need to be putting some money away for this. How much you pay will depend on your income.

You can also make voluntary repayments to the Australian Taxation Office (ATO) at any time. But it's important to focus on paying off bad debt first. It doesn't make sense to try to clear your HECS/HELP if you have a credit card, especially if you're in a lower tax bracket and may not need to pay any HECS/HELP that year.

As with any other debt, your HECS/HELP loan will be compounding over time, although this is still at a very low rate compared to most other forms of credit like credit cards and Buy Now Pay Laters. While there is no interest payable on your HELP debt, however, it is 'indexed to inflation' which means the debt is raised each year in line with the cost of living. The indexation is added to your debt on 1 June each year. In 2022 the indexation factor was 3.9% so if your loan was $10,000 it would increase to $10,390.

The dangers of credit cards

Credit cards should come with a warning – 'I will burn you!' Seriously, I think anyone who gets a credit card should have to do a quiz to say they understand how these slippery little suckers work. Why? Because they have been designed for one reason, and the answer isn't to help you manage your money – it's to make banks and credit card companies more money. You are paying for the privilege to borrow someone else's money.

With a credit card, your money is negatively compounding (which is the opposite to what it does when you invest your money).

My friend Meg always looked like she was living her best life. She rented a fabulous apartment in the eastern suburbs of Sydney by herself, was always having drinks, endless brunches, weekends away with friends – if we went for sushi she would get the black plates (OMG, I know). I just assumed she was doing really well and earning good money.

Much later I found out that she was in serious credit card debt, and when she didn't get the pay rise she had expected her reality came crashing down. She was shocked the day she added all her credit cards and Buy Now Pay Laters together to find out she had racked up over $20,000 of debt.

From then on she tracked her spending and lived on a cash budget. She withdrew $100 cash for 'discretionary' spending each week to cover everything outside of food, rent, transport, utilities. She also moved apartments and reduced her rent by $660 a month. She started making her own lunch and opting out of weekends away and long brunches, opting instead for walks and trips to galleries. She was surprised that her social life didn't change too much. In total it took her 18 months to become debt-free.

Financial coach Betsy Westcott says people with credit card debt have generally either 'eaten it, drunk it or holidayed it' but they find it hard to recall where the money was spent. It's almost always on wants not needs.

Let's take a quick look at how easy it is to get into a debt cycle.

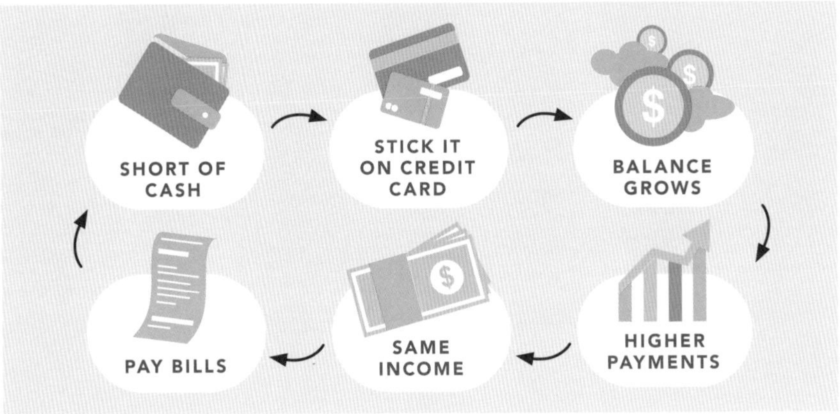

Jackie is starting at university and she needs to buy a few things for her college room. It comes to a total of $500. If she uses her credit card she will receive a statement telling her the total amount due, the minimum payment due and when her payment is due. Jackie can do two things:

1. Pay the credit card off in full.
2. Pay the minimum amount on or before the due date.

If Jackie goes with option 1 and pays the total amount by the due date she will pay no interest. If she only pays the minimum amount it will take her two years and eight months to pay off $500, and she would pay over $131 in interest repayments (with an 18% annual percentage rate). As you get closer to zero your minimum repayments are reduced which might seem good but means you pay more interest overall (they really don't want to lose your business).

Other things to be aware of:

- Annual fees.
- Annual Percentage Rate (APR) – the interest rate you pay on the money you borrow per year. Reserve Bank of Australia (RBA) data

shows that the average standard credit card interest rate is 19.94%.

- Foreign Transaction fee – if you use the card internationally.
- Cash advances – if you use a credit card to withdraw cash you'll be hit with a much higher rate and it cancels any 0% promotional balance rate you might have been on.
- Billing cycle – the length of time between the last statement closing date and the next. If you don't pay off your debt in full, then from the start of the next cycle any remaining debt accrues interest until you have paid it off.

Here's an example to illustrate the dangers of billing cycles because they get complicated:

On 1 June Anne pops to the shops and buys a TV for $500 and TV sideboard for $250, putting both on credit card. The end of the statement period is 30 June. The due date for the minimum monthly repayment (MMR) or the balance in full (in this case $750) is 25 July.

If Anne pays the full balance on 25 July, then the statement period commencing 1 July will be interest-free. If only the MMR is paid on 25 July then there will be no interest-free period commencing 1 July.

If Anne does a cash advance on 1 June to pay for the goods, there is NO interest-free period on that withdrawal, and it will attract interest (often at a higher rate) until it's paid off in full.

Buy Now Pay Later (BNPLs)

Remember them 'good ol' days' when if you really wanted something, you saved for it and then you got it, well, let me introduce you to layby's evil stepsister – Buy Now Pay Later.

These are the new kids on the block and, although they have cool ads and pretty celebrities endorsing them, they can be dangerous. Unlike layby, no credit checks are done when it comes to BNPLs. And, oh my word, there are as many different types of BNPL as there are dating apps – Afterpay, Zip, Humm, Klarna, Beforepay, the list goes on (around 20 at the time of writing this book). They are growing in popularity: 60% of Aussies surveyed said they had used a BNPL, which was higher than both the UK and USA.

I've been asked a few times by PR companies if I would promote BNPL companies to my audience, to which I respond I am in the business of helping women get out of debt, not get into it! I then delete that and reply, 'That company does not align with our LFC values.'

How does BNPL work?

Mel goes into a Nike shop to buy some activewear. She finds a cute li'l matching top-and-bottoms totalling $272 and there's a little Afterpay logo so she gets out her app, she 'Afterpays it' and pays only $68 (25% of the total amount) and walks out of the shop. Afterpay has now bought the debt from the retailer at a discounted rate (one way they make their money) and Mel then pays back Afterpay in four instalments over eight weeks. If she pays it back on time, no qualms, but if something comes up then she'll be hit with a late fee (that's the other way they make their money). Let's say Mel doesn't get paid or something comes up and she can't make the repayments. If she was to miss all four payments she would owe an additional $68, the equivalent of 25% interest, which is higher than the average credit card interest of around 18 to 19%.

Even one of the biggest BNPLs says on its website 'no external credit checks, no interest, no fees when you pay on time', with the keywords being *pay on time*. Don't pay on time and you will be hit with a late fee.

What's even scarier is you can now buy now and pay later for restaurant meals, school fees, there's even talk of being able to use them to cover your rent, which means people will be in this debt trap forever. Lisa Simpson sees some people paying for their BNPLs on their credit cards and then also getting charged interest there, as well as some people using BNPL to buy everyday groceries. You can see how Aussies are getting caught up in a whirlwind of debt at really young ages.

My beef with the whole BNPL thing is:

1. They are easy to access as you don't need a credit check, which means they prey on people in lower socioeconomic positions who might not typically be approved.
2. They target young women.
3. They don't come under the same protections as other financial institutions, and it's harder to report on their behaviour to the ombudsman (Australian Financial Complaints Authority, AFCA). Some BNPLs are starting to voluntarily become members of AFCA though, which is good for consumers.
4. We are breeding a generation of people reliant on debt.

A recent ASIC report found that one in five consumers surveyed said that, in the last 12 months, they had missed or were late paying other bills in order to make their BNPL payments on time.

Lisa Simpson, our resident debt counsellor, says that when she examines her clients' bank accounts she is seeing a pattern of eight to ten different BNPL companies alongside payday lenders and other small amount credit contracts. People are using these for everything from Christmas presents to groceries! But alongside all the BNPL payments are multiple missed payments, which impacts the clients' credit score, and keeps them in a cycle of debt.

Lisa suggests that if this is you, speak to a financial counsellor or a money coach who can assist you in looking at your budget and working out how to live 'within your income'. With multiple debts, a financial counsellor may be able to discuss other options such as payment plans with no fees, moratoriums on payments until circumstances improve, and other options.

That's a wrap!

If you're struggling with debt there is always help available. Kristen Hartnett from Moneycare, a service provided by the Salvos, says they see people who are in debt from $1 to $1 million and everyone is welcome.

Don't be afraid. Debt is easy to get into and much harder to get out of, but there are plenty of strategies you can use to make it manageable. Give the avalanche or snowball method a go but if you are still struggling call the National Debt Helpline – 1800 007 007 (think James Bond!) – where you can talk to a debt counsellor. You can also speak to someone at Moneycare or Good Shepherd.

To action with your gal pals

- ☐ Follow the avalanche or snowball method for any high interest debt.
- ☐ Speak to a debt counsellor (free) or a money coach (paid) if you need extra support.

CHAPTER 6

When Shit Happens

You've got your $1000 sitting in your OMG fund ready for any small emergencies but what happens when life throws big curveballs your way? Pow, pow, pow.

We're all aware of how devastating recent times have been between Covid and the effects of climate change. We need to make sure that we are protected in the event of an emergency, a natural disaster, losing our job or getting sick. You know how they tell you on a plane to 'put on your own mask first before assisting others'? This chapter is all about making sure you have your mask on because you'll then be in a much better position to help your family and friends! We will be chatting about must-have insurances, wills and how to disaster-proof your money, and also the cost around putting your eggs on ice! The #Adulting continues.

Essential insurance

I know you're thinking, 'Insurance! Excuse-snooze me, I'm busy poking my eye out with a fork.' Yes, talking about insurance might not be on the top of your list of sexy topics to discuss but let's make a deal: I'll just take you through the ones that our experts say are really important.

These are the main ones to consider:

- Home and contents insurance
- Income protection insurance
- Car insurance
- Health insurance
- Travel insurance

HOW INSURANCE WORKS

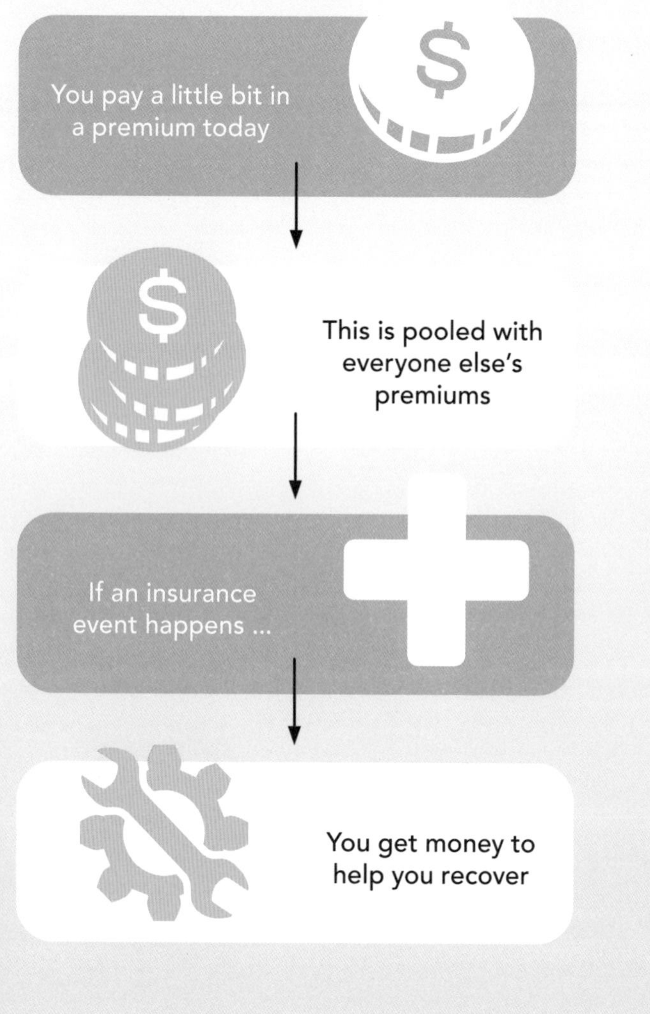

Home and contents insurance

If you have a mortgage, having house insurance is non-negotiable. Many people don't realise that if their house is damaged or destroyed by fire, if they have no home insurance, they will still have to repay the bank the full mortgage for a house that no longer exists.

According to the Australian Securities and Investments Commission (ASIC) up to 80% of homeowners are underinsured – that's a hell of a lot.

When selecting your home insurance, there are two types:

Total replacement cover will cover the cost to rebuild your home to how it was before a disaster.

Sum-insured cover will cover your home to a set amount as selected by you.

Before choosing a policy, get quotes for at least two policies. Look at what would be covered, what isn't covered and any caps or limits before you settle on one.

If you are renting, you may want to consider having contents insurance. This covers the things that you own within the home.

See, that wasn't so painful.

Income protection insurance

I always ask people what their most valuable asset is. People say things like my home, my car, my phone, my smile, my jewellery, my super … but the answer is you!

Insurance broker and LFC ambassador Marnie Maloney says, 'You are your MVP (most valuable asset) and you need protecting. Taking out a home loan or starting a family are often triggers for women to start thinking about life insurance, but the truth is, from the moment you join the workforce, your ability to earn an income is your most valuable asset.'

And this is true even if you think you don't earn that much. As Marnie puts it, if you're on $60,000 a year for the next 30 years that will be over $1.8 million. If you had an ATM in your lounge room that you could take $60,000 out of a year, would you consider getting that insured? I think so. This is the idea of income protection insurance. It insures you and your ability to earn money.

In Australia, 83% of us insure our car, and yet only 31% of us insure our income. Income protection insurance is a way to look after yourself, pay rent and buy groceries, and can be purchased either privately or through your super fund (see Chapter 7).

The cost of income protection insurance ranges depending on your age and health history. The good news is that life insurance companies see young people as relatively low risk. If you're young and healthy, premiums are cheap.

Life insurance

Here's a snapshot of the main life insurances you might want to think about.

- Life cover (death cover) should really be called death insurance because it pays your family a lump sum when you die.
- Total and permanent disability (TPD) pays a lump sum that can help with repaying debts, as well as things like rehabilitation and living costs, if you become totally and permanently disabled because of illness or injury.
- Trauma insurance covers you if you're diagnosed with a serious illness or major injury such as cancer, a heart condition, head injury or stroke. This is the only one you can't hold through your super.

Car insurance

Lisa Simpson sees many people with debts ranging from $5000 to $90,000 simply because they did not take out car insurance. They've been involved in an accident, they've damaged their own or another person's car, home or fence, and they have to pay for those damages. If this happens to you and you can't pay, insurance companies will have a debt collector pursue you doggedly for that money. They won't care if you're only on a Centrelink income, they just want you to pay for the damages that you have caused. And if you do own anything, such as a house, they can ask the court for permission to sell your house so that they can retrieve any money for damages.

Let's break car insurance types down because they used to really confuse me too!

Compulsory third party (CTP)

Everyone has to have compulsory third party insurance (it's in the name – compulsory). It's also known as green slip insurance or a transport accident charge depending on what state you're in. You generally pay this when you renew your car registration. It provides compensation for people injured or killed when your vehicle is involved in an accident.

Comprehensive insurance (the OG of car insurance)

If you can afford it, comprehensive car insurance is going to give you the most protection. This covers you and the other car or thing that you have hit. Whether you have an accident on the motorway and hit a car or a series of cars, or you knock out a fence or a light pole or damage your car, comprehensive insurance covers everything. As a result, it's a little bit more expensive. If you have a loan on your car you should have comprehensive insurance, because you don't want to have an accident where your car is completely written off and you are still paying for it for the next five years – sadly this happens.

Third-party fire and theft

This covers the other car or property that you have damaged in a crash, but it doesn't cover damage to your car. Your car may not be worth insurance, but you want to make sure that if you hit a Mercedes-Benz you will be covered. As the name suggests, it also covers limited fire and theft damage to your car.

Third-party property

This covers any other vehicle or property that you have damaged, but it doesn't cover your own vehicle. It's the most affordable, and the one Lisa recommends if you can't afford anything else. She says, 'I've seen people with up to $90,000 worth of debt, which if they had just paid $200 a year for third-party insurance, they wouldn't have.'

Health insurance

We are very privileged in this country to have a public system that will look after us if we get sick. It is called Medicare and it gives Aussies access to a range of healthcare services for free or at a lower cost. Australia also has a private health system.

The Medicare levy – To help fund Medicare, most taxpayers contribute 2% of their taxable income, unless they earn under a certain amount, in which case they don't need to pay anything at all.

Medicare Levy Surcharge (MLS) – This charge was brought in to encourage people who can afford it to take out private patient hospital cover and reduce demand on the public system. If your annual income is over $90,000 as a single (or $180,000 as a couple, family or single parent) you may have to pay the Medicare Levy Surcharge, ranging up to 1.5% of your taxable income, if you and your dependents don't have the appropriate level of private hospital cover.

Use a Medicare Levy Surcharge calculator to find out how this affects you.

Private health insurance

There are two components to private health insurance.

Hospital cover: helps to cover some of your costs if you need to go to the hospital.

Extras cover: helps to cover the costs of services not always covered by Medicare, including dental, optical, physiotherapy and chiropractic services.

Work out what you need and if you can save money by getting a basic hospital cover. It's also worth checking to see if you need ambulance cover in your state. Some states such as Queensland have free ambulance cover, but if your state doesn't you could end up with a hefty charge if you ever need an ambo.

Travel insurance

We have all heard a horror story or two of people travelling and losing their luggage or passport, being robbed, getting sick or getting stuck in some kind of disaster. Travel insurance policies cover you for emergencies or accidents that might happen to you or your belongings while you are overseas or on holiday, or just away from your home. It'll cover things such as medical expenses, natural disasters, trip cancellations and delays, car hire, terrorism and lost luggage.

Things to check:

- Some activities like cruises or winter sports (skiing, snowboarding) won't be covered by regular travel insurance policies so you might need to get these added on.
- If you're pregnant and travelling you might need to get coverage for pre-existing conditions or upgrade your policy.
- Some policies exclude the US so check it includes the countries you're visiting.

- Check the Covid clause – not all travel insurance policies will provide cover around COVID-19.

You might eye roll when I say read the product disclosure statement (PDS), but it's definitely worth having a read through. (I always think these are the least boring of the PDSs out there!)

What about insuring your furry friends?

If your pet is young with no pre-existing conditions then insurance could definitely be considered. If you opt out of getting pet insurance make sure you put money aside in your OMG fund or set up your own pet OMG fund for if little Bella gets sick.

Ladies, listen up!

Put those babies on ice

I'm a 30-something-year-old single lady (woohoo) and I want to have kids one day. I haven't met the right person who I want to settle down with yet (if you're reading this and have a nice brother, hook me up). I try not to feel the pressure but sometimes when I look at my married friends or the fact that Bindi Irwin has a kid, I get a little panicky. I know I shouldn't but I do.

That's why this year I'm booking in to get my eggs put on ice! It's a great option for women to increase their chances of conceiving later in life (and it's going to keep my mum very happy).

Many of my friends have been, or are going through, this process. It's smart, but it does need to be budgeted for which is why I wanted to include it in this section. If this is a path you want to take (and I completely understand if it's not) you don't want to miss out on this opportunity because of money.

The best approach is to have an initial discussion and fertility assessment with your GP and then a referral to a specialist to explore all the options.

The cost of treatment will depend on whether your treatment is covered by Medicare and whether you have private health insurance. Many fertility providers also offer low-cost treatment options if you meet certain criteria, like if you have endometriosis for example. This can mean significant savings for you. Fertility companies offer egg freezing for around $5000 plus medication and anaesthetist fees, and charge $35–$50 per month for egg storage. Freezing her eggs after a divorce, my good friend and international entrepreneur Annie Johnson said she felt an overwhelming sense of relief and control in her life. 'As much as possible, I was "buying time" ... time to find the right partner and time to have a family later in my life.'

Top up your OMG fund

We talked earlier in the book about creating your OMG fund, with $1000 for those OMG moments life throws your way. Now you've done that, let's boost your emergency stash with three to six months' worth of expenses. If you're single and you rent, three months will do the trick. If you have a family or own a home or business, you want to be aiming for closer to six months.

Why you really need a will

Do you *really* need a will, I hear you ask? As WillPro founder Elisabeth Woodward says, 'If you're (a) alive; and (b) over the age of 18, congratulations! You're officially part of the needing-a-will club!'

Nothing quite says you're an adult like 'Have you thought about your death yet?' It's a grim topic but doing a will is actually a really selfless thing to do. There's a big chance at some point in your life you will die – in fact, I'd bet my life on it (okay, I'll stop with the dad jokes – just trying to lighten the mood).

Without a will you're in the hands of the court, which means that your wishes might not be carried out the way you want them to be. For a few hundred dollars (or less), depending on your situation, it's really worth getting that sorted!

Jargon schmargon

A **will or last testament** is a legal document outlining how your assets will be distributed after your death. It is the only way to ensure that your assets will be dealt with the way you want them to be.

People get weird when it comes to money, especially families, and we can all recall a story where Aunt Marg hasn't spoken to Uncle Frank for the last 20 years because there was a fight over money. By getting a will done you're not only saving money, because there won't be extra legal fees, you're reducing the risk of awkward family Christmases for years to come. #WorthIt

WILL	VS	NO WILL
 You decide who gets what.		 A court-appointed administrator decides who gets what.
 You choose who the guardians of your children/pets will be.		 A court-appointed administrator makes decisions regarding the care of your children/pets.
 Your money goes where and to whom you want it to.		 The money in your estate is funnelled into legal fees and potenial beneficaries will get whatever is left over.
 Your executor applies for 'probate' (approval of your will by the courts) and can then begin to administer your estate in line with your wishes.		 Your Estate is 'frozen' and intestacy laws now apply. Any person (known or unknown to you) can apply to become the court-appointed administrator of your estate.

A good time to get a will, or update an old one, is if you are:

- Ending a relationship (separation and divorce)
- Getting married
- Becoming a financial dependent
- A beneficiary with a disability
- Starting or buying a business
- Unwell, especially if you have a terminal diagnosis
- Moving overseas (big tax consequences!)
- Receiving an inheritance
- Purchasing or selling property

If you think you have nothing of value, think again. You will still have assets in your superannuation, and your life insurance can often be a significant amount.

Melbourne-based Estate Planner Lucy Pearcy says, 'If a person dies without a will in Australia, they are declared to have died "intestate". In these cases, the state will determine what happens according to the laws of intestacy. These laws vary greatly from state to state. During intestacy proceedings, any person may apply to be appointed as the administrator of another's estate, and this can include an individual (e.g. friend, partner, relative, ex-partner) or even an external third party, such as a lawyer or government administrator.'

Traditionally, law firms will charge anywhere from between $500 to $1000 for a standard will. There are online companies that now offer affordable personalised standard wills (written by their team of lawyers) from around $99, but if your situation is complicated it is worth seeking out an estate planner. It's also worth noting your super doesn't make up part of your estate (I know right – who makes these confusing laws?) so we'll show you how to sort that in the next chapter.

We suggest you skip the DIY post office wills. This is an area of law that crosses over with so many other areas of law – property, family, corporate, super – and you don't get a second shot at it! Leaving any problems to the courts to fix is extremely expensive, so the upfront investment is worth it for peace of mind and certainty.

That's a wrap!

No one ever wants to think something bad is going to happen to them. My sister never thought she would ever get cancer, but it can happen, and if it were to ever happen to you – whether that be an accident or illness – you don't want to have to be worrying about money or about paying your bills. A few small actions now can mean you and your future (and your family) are protected. Do these things and I can assure you your future self will send you a big high five!

To action with your gal pals

- ☐ Do an insurance review (have you got enough cover?).
- ☐ Work out if you need private health insurance.
- ☐ Top up your OMG fund.
- ☐ Complete and sign a will.

CHAPTER 7

Get Super Savvy

'I should probably put more money into my super fund,' said nobody ever.

Let's face it, when we hear the word superannuation it's easy for us to switch off and think about last night's episode of *The Bach*. I mean, retirement … it's just so faaaaaar awaaaaay! That's a future Molly problem, right?

It's easy to think it will all work out but I have seen the stats and they don't lie! We are living longer and earning less, resulting in poor outcomes for women in retirement. According to an Industry Super Australia study, 70% of retired single women live on the pension and 40% of retired single women live below the poverty line.

Yes, the super system was designed by men for men and there are some big systemic issues at work, some of which need to change, but right now we have a few steps you can take so your super fund will be looking as good as J.Lo at 50 #HotDamn!

I get it, when you're in your twenties, thirties and even forties, superannuation is a topic that's hard to connect with. I mean, I'm trying to tackle Tinder not my retirement – I've got a non-existent wedding, honeymoon and family to plan for (or you might even have a real one). Christina Hobbs, CEO and co-founder of Verve Super, Australia's first super fund tailored for women, says, 'I remember being 18 and glancing at the "superannuation line" on my payslip and not knowing what it was – thinking it was a tax or something. Even when I realised that this was compulsory savings for my retirement I still felt like the money belonged to someone else and the decision of which super fund was up to my employer. When we're young the concept of retirement seems so far away and that line on our payslip is so easy to ignore.'

Plus they haven't made it easy, right? I have opened a letter from my super provider, understood nothing and stuck it straight in the drawer (*cough*, bin). And I'm not alone. Only one in three Aussie women are certain or have a good idea how much they'll need for retirement, and 44% of women rely on their partner's income as the main source of funds for retirement. And the grimmest stat of all: 40% of older single retired women live in poverty. Imagine getting to retirement and being homeless! We must do better as a nation but, for now, you can start taking immediate action.

Let's say you're earning $75,000 per year and someone came up and said, 'Hey, give me $750,' and they took this money every single month. You would be like, 'Hey, whatcha doing with my money?'

This is *exactly* what's happening with our super. Yet we don't think of it as our money and we don't ask enough questions.

The ATO estimates there is just under $14 billion of lost super just sitting there waiting to be claimed (and, yes, we will show you how to check if any of those sweet dollar bills are yours).

We are going to do a quick mindset reset. Every time you see the word 'superannuation' I want you to think 'Future Freedom Fund' or 'Frickin' Big Holiday Fund' because that's essentially what it is. Imagine getting to your holiday and realising that you've got no money to spend. 😱

We don't make enough decisions with the future in mind so to get on top of your super you're going to have to fight natural instinct!

Imagine if we treated our cars like we did our super.

Where did you park it? *Ummmm, not sure.*

How much is it worth? *Eeeeeeee?*

Got insurance? *No idea.*

What brand is it? *Stop attacking me!*

What is super?

Put super simply, super is your money that is put away now (in a super fund) for later (retirement). It's really important to remember this is *your* money. It's like your money is being put into a safe but the safe only opens when you hit preservation age. Most people can access their super from age 60 but it will vary slightly depending on when you were born. You can't touch it until you get to that magic retirement age unless you meet some pretty intense circumstances (none of which are good). Once that money hits your super it's there for the long term (which is a good thing: we want to keep our greasy little mitts off it and let compounding do its thing #GrowBabyGrow!).

The safe (your super fund) invests your money into the stock market and different asset classes and it grows over time. Yippee! And did you know that you can actually choose where it's invested and how much risk you want to take on?

At LFC events I'll ask people to put their hands up if they invest, and very few people put their hands up, so then I say, 'Hands up if you have super' (to which everyone puts their hands up), and then I like to have an Oprah moment: 'You're an investor, you're an investor – you're all investors!'

Tax talk

You also get some great tax benefits when you contribute to your super because (drum roll) it's a tax structure, which is why it's even more important we utilise it! Many of us are being taxed 32% to 37% of our pay, whereas the money you contribute to superannuation gets taxed at a concessional rate of 15% (this does increase to 30% when you are earning over $250,000 per year). And you can contribute more to your superannuation to bring your tax rate down, keeping more of your hard-earned money in future you's pocket.

Not only can you potentially reduce your taxable income with tax-effective contributions (known as concessional contributions), the earnings on your fund also only get taxed at that concessional rate (15% or 30%).

5 steps to getting super savvy

Step 1 Find your super

Firstly, if you are over 18 and have earned more than $450 in a month then it's extremely likely you will already have a super fund as you would have been automatically signed up when you started working. You might also find that you have lots of different super funds from part-time jobs when you were younger, like that time you worked at Macca's or Woolies.

(Note that in 2022 the government scrapped the $450 superannuation guarantee threshold, so you don't have to earn over $450 a month to get paid super, which will be very beneficial to women.)

If you're employed, your employer should be paying at least 10% of your earnings into your super account. The keyword is *your* super. This minimum payment is called the super guarantee or the SG (which I think sounds cooler!). And the great news: the SG is set to slowly increase each year to 12% by 2025.

Imagine if you walked past $500 on the street that had your name on it and you didn't pick it up! That's the same as not claiming your lost super. The good news is there is an easy way to do this through the government's myGov website.

This will take you ten minutes so go do it now!

How to find your lost super!

1. Login to myGov (finding your password will be the most time-consuming part).
2. Once you have logged in, on your myGov dashboard click 'Link another service'.
3. Click 'Australian Tax Office' under the 'Link a service' section.
4. Click on 'Manage my super' to see the details of all your super funds.

You can also call the lost super search line 13 28 65. You'll need your tax file number (TFN). This is the number you get when you start your first job, and it's with you for life.

Step 2 Are you on track?

It's time to make sure you're on track for the lifestyle you know you want (ding, cue champagne – that style of retirement).

When people ask if they are contributing enough the answer is most commonly no (call me psychic).

The Association of Superannuation Funds of Australia (ASFA) estimates that for a comfortable retirement, a couple who own their own home should have $640,000 at retirement (assuming they are 67 years old) and $545,000 for singles. That might work for most people, but will it work for you? What do you want your retirement to look like?

How do you work out if you're putting enough away? And if you're on track? Check out this table:

GENDER	AGE	AVERAGE BALANCE	BALANCE REQUIRED TODAY FOR A COMFORTABLE RETIREMENT	GAP
Women	30	$22,850	$61,000	**-$38,150**
	40	$54,765	$154,000	**-$99,235**
	50	$101,560	$271,000	**-$169,440**
	60	$165,986	$430,000	**-$264,014**

Source: www.canstar.com.au – 21/06/2021. Average balances based on those reported in the APRA Annual Superannuation Bulletin (June 2020).

If you're thinking, '*Holy hell!* How am I meant to come up with that kind of dosh?' Well, if you want a million dollars at retirement, it doesn't mean you need to contribute a million dollars!

Let me introduce you to my friend and your friend-to-be, *compounding returns*. We will go into this in a lot of detail in Chapter 8 but basically compounding returns is when our money is making money.

Confused?

Let's work through an example. Amy is 35 and she's a corporate lawyer earning $100,000 (I know this isn't a realistic number for some people but it makes it easier for example purposes). She currently has a super balance of $50,000. Amy's employer pays the standard 2022/2023 SG of 10.5%. Let's assume she gets a 7.5% return on her fund each year and has an annual investment fee of 1%.

Let's look at what Amy would end up with at 65:

Estimated super balance = $505,380

Fees paid = $104,269

Now, what would happen if we changed just one thing? Let's say the fund returned 9.5% and there was still a fee of 1%. Amy would retire with $714,293.

Visit superratings.com.au/top-10-super-funds to check out the average performance of the top ten balanced super funds over a five-year period.

I'm self-employed – HELP!

Oh, the joys of running your own gig! But let's bust a myth I hear all the time around super and the self-employed: 'My business is my retirement.' We can't rely on this, for numerous reasons. What if the next Covid hits, can your business survive that? Or what if a big competitor comes along? You need to be paying yourself minimum 10–12% – set it up so it automatically goes from your account to your super fund each month. It takes minutes to do this and your future self will thank you big time. If I had to manually do this each month, it would never get done.

I talk to a lot of women who run their own business and don't pay themselves super because it's not compulsory, and it means they end up in tricky situations in retirement. We don't want that for you! We all need to get into better habits of paying ourselves super. You can have your cake and eat it too.

How to boost your super

If you're not on track, it's never too late to turn things around. The government wants us to save for our retirement and encourages it through lots of different incentives. It's like they knew we would be bad at saving for the future and don't want to support our broke butts through retirement! Here are ways to boost your super:

Concessional contributions (contributing more before tax)

These are before-tax contributions and are limited to the concessional contribution cap each year, which was $27,500 for the 2022/2023 financial year. What your employer pays (the SG) and what you salary sacrifice yourself count towards this, as do any deductible contributions you make (more on this shortly). The benefit? These contributions are taxed at 15% (or 30% if you earn over $250,000 per year).

Here's an example of the difference they can make:

Two friends Loz and Claire are both 30, earning $75,000 a year. Loz's employer pays the standard SG 10.5% and she doesn't contribute anything extra.

Claire is also paid the standard SG 10.5% plus she puts an extra 5% in each month. The investments perform exactly the same but Claire retires with $160,000 more than Loz. A small amount now can make a big difference later. Work out what your own retirement fund would be if you contibuted extra at moneysmart.gov.au.

Non-concessional contributions

These are voluntary after-tax contributions, so the money you put into your superannuation from your pay or savings after tax has already been taken out. These contributions are limited to $110,000 per year for 2021/2022. You may also consider claiming a tax deduction on some of these contributions, which converts them from being 'non-concessional' into 'concessional' – talk to your super fund about this as it's important to understand the implications and the relevant contribution caps.

Catch-up concessional contributions

If your superannuation balance is under $500,000, your unused concessional contribution cap since 2018/2019 will be accrued and can be carried forward up to five years for use in future years – this is called 'catch-up concessional contributions'. This means if you didn't use your whole concessional cap one year in that period, it's not wasted. To check if you have any 'catch up' available, login to myGov and check in the ATO section, or ask your super fund.

Government co-contribution

If you're earning less than $57,016 for the 2022/2023 financial year and make a non-concessional contribution to your super you may be eligible for the government co-contribution. This is a free little boost of up to $500 into your superannuation.

Spouse contributions and contribution splitting

If you're taking time out of the workforce (e.g. to look after kids) your super shouldn't have to suffer. If you have a partner you should discuss how you can work together to keep your super on track like making spouse contributions or splitting super contributions. Spouse contributions will potentially mean your partner gets a tax offset for putting money into your super. And super splitting is when a portion of the super contributions your partner receives gets transferred into your super. Like all of the different types of contributions, there are a few conditions and limits, so talk to your super fund or get personal financial advice for your situation. Fun fact: all super funds have advisors that work for them, so book in your free call!

Super Rewards

Super Rewards is a cashback site for future you. Yes, please! Similar to the cashback sites we discussed in Chapter 2, you get cash back but it automatically gets put into your nominated super fund. Nice!

Super consolidation

Trenna Probert, the founder of Super Fierce, says having more than one super fund is like having multiple phone plans for one mobile phone. You wouldn't pay Telstra, Optus and Vodafone for three separate plans when you only have one mobile phone! So, why would you pay for more than one super account?

Thinking of a consolidation?

The pros:

- Simplicity! Less paperwork and much easier to remember where it is.
- Less fees! Most funds have fixed admin fees so the more funds you have, the more you pay.
- Save on insurance! If you have a few funds, chances are you're paying for a few insurance policies that you may not need.

The cons:

- Consolidating your super might mean that you get rid of insurance policies without realising it. I've heard horror stories of people getting sick a year later only to find out they accidentally got rid of all their insurance when they consolidated. Talk to your super funds or get advice to see what you might be saying goodbye to!

Christina Hobbs says, 'I spoke to a woman once who told me that she had "sorting her super out" as a New Year's resolution for five years in a row, and then realised that it only took her 20 minutes one afternoon to do some research and consolidate her eight super accounts. But that five year delay ended up costing her thousands of dollars in double fees and lost returns.'

Step 3 Know your fees

Not sure what fees you're paying? You're not alone! The statements can be très confusing and there's sometimes a bazillion fees. I personally think it's easier to call your fund and ask them to list out all of the fees you pay each year as a dollar amount and then what that is as a percentage amount.

Check whether the fees are transparent and low cost, as well as good value. (Don't be fooled by low investment fees – look for admin fees, performance fees and indirect fees. They have lots of names to help hide them.)

According to financial comparison website Canstar, on average, people in the 'default investment option' of a super fund pay between 0.88% to 1.24% of their account balance in fees per year, depending on their age and super balance. Check out what fees you're paying and then compare your fund's performance to some of the lower fee funds. Ultimately, you shouldn't be paying higher fees if your fund is not outperforming the market.

A fee of 1% might not sound like a lot but the difference between 1% and 2% can be a lot of money over a lifetime.

Remember Amy from our earlier example? If Amy had paid 2% in fees instead of 1%, she would have paid over $100,000 worth of fees (that's at least five super posh cruises)!

Step 4 Is your super performing like J.Lo?

We want your fund performing as good as Jenny from the Block! Your investments are not going to return an 8% flat return every year – some years it might be more, others it will be less, that's how averages work. But we want to make sure we aren't paying for an underperformer. Head over to the government super comparison website YourSuper and look up your fund's performance compared to others. If it's low then consider breaking up with your super fund. #ItsYouNotMe

If you decide you want to break up with your super fund then make sure in your next fund:

- You are comfortable in terms of your risk tolerance as well as values.
- They have a track record of good performance.
- They will provide you with the insurance you need. Always check this out *before* you leave your old fund and insurance.

Do you know where your super is being invested?

If you have no idea what your super is invested into, you're not alone. When you start a job you're so focused on imposter syndrome, remembering where the bathroom is, working out what your actual role is and realising it's different to what they hired you to do … there's a lot going on, so it's okay if you missed the 'Where your super is invested' session they didn't provide to you.

Three in five Aussie workers say their super fund was picked by their employer. This is called a default fund and has traditionally been lumped into what's called a 'balanced fund' (imagine there is a scale of low risk to high risk – balanced is supposed to be about the middle of the road but it is often on the higher side of the risk scale, and there isn't a lot of consistency between super funds). The good news is you have a lot of control over this if you want it, and in most circumstances, it's as easy as looking at what other investment options your super fund offers, and filling out a form to change.

Types of investments:

- Growth
- High Growth
- Balanced (usually the default)
- Conservative
- Cash
- Ethical

An ethical option can sit anywhere on the risk spectrum – from high growth to conservative. This option aims to screen out investments in companies that don't meet certain environmental, social and governance standards. Ethical investing is becoming more popular and more accessible.

Christina Hobbs says, 'There's so many women who use a keep cup, always take reusable bags to the supermarket yet at the same time may have their money invested through their super in fossil fuel companies, tobacco companies, gambling operators and other nasties. The good news is that research by the Responsible Investment Association of Australia is showing that ethical funds have actually outperformed the market over the short, medium and long term in Australia – so there's no reason to compromise values for returns.' If this is something important to you, make sure you check with your super fund what their ethical options are. The criteria for 'ethical' can change from fund to fund.

The time frame of your investment is a factor when considering volatility risk. While cash has been steady over the last 20 years, it's also grown less than assets like shares. If your savings are growing too slowly, they might not keep up with the rising costs of living (inflation).

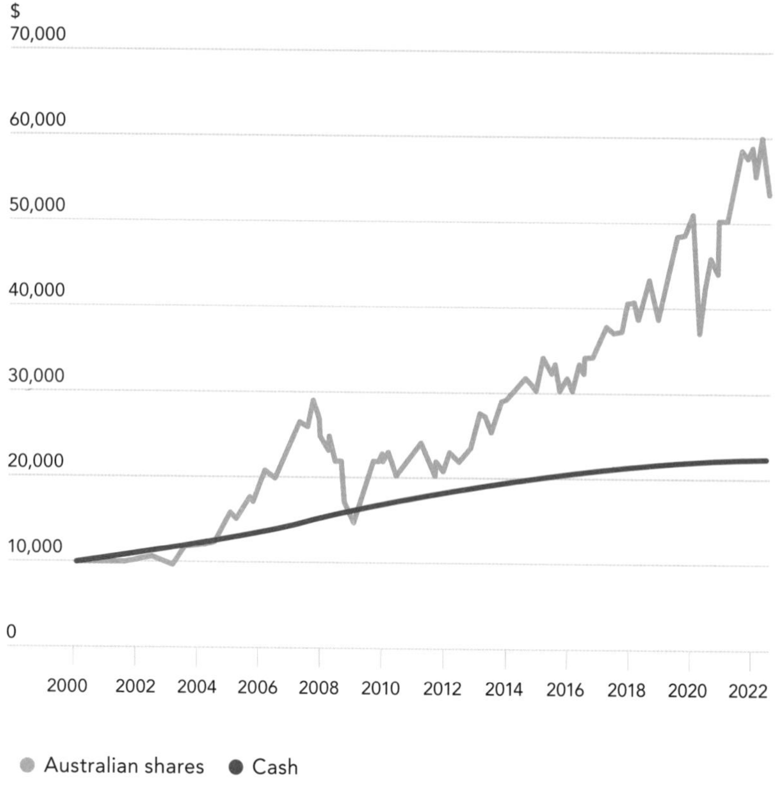

The information in this graph has been prepared using data from the Vanguard Digital Index Chart. Vanguard Investments Australia Ltd ABN 72 072 881 086 AFSL 227263. Jan 2000 – August 2022

Typically, higher growth funds will have historically returned higher over the long term and will target higher long-term returns, but they are also more likely to experience short-term volatility when the markets are rocky. Understanding which of these best suits your needs and your risk profile will help you compare the right type of option for you across different funds. If you aren't familiar with these terms, or don't know which risk profile may be best for you, then check out the Australian Government's Moneysmart website for more information.

The general rule of thumb is the younger you are, the more risk you can take because you have a longer time period (20 years or more) for your investments to ride the rollercoaster short-term ups and downs. Whereas, your mother or grandmother who is already retired and now relying on her money to live off might want to be more conservative so her returns aren't as volatile.

Grab your super statement or login and have a look how your superannuation is invested.

1. Go to the investment section on your super fund's website and look at what investments they offer, the allocation of what is in each investment, the risk associated with that investment (usually presented as a scale) and suggested time frame.
2. Want to make a switch? You can transfer your balance to a new fund by contacting the new fund directly and they will arrange it for you, or you can use the ATO rollover form. Don't forget to tell your employer.
3. And, as always, if you're not sure – get advice.

Step 5 Stay protected

Insurance in super definitely has its perks – for one thing, the premiums don't affect your cashflow. But keep in mind, future you is paying for these. Knowing what cover you have and what you are paying is important – just like you don't want to be underinsured, you don't want to be paying for something you don't need.

Typically, you can have three types of personal insurance within superannuation:

Death Insurance (also known as Life Insurance): a lump sum payment paid to your beneficiary when you pass away. It is also often paid to you if you are diagnosed with a terminal illness.

Total and Permanent Disability Insurance: Usually a lump sum given if you are unable to work again due to illness or injury. I say 'usually' as some super funds have changed this from a one-off lump sum to partial payment instalments over a few years. Each super fund will have different terms and conditions so make sure you're familiar with yours.

Salary Continuance (also known as Income Protection): Salary Continuance protects your income if you're unable to work due to being sick or injured. This could be short term like three months, or potentially until your expected retirement age. It's designed to provide up to 85% of your pre-disability income to make sure you can meet your living expenses. The waiting period (how long you have to be off work before you can claim) and the benefit period (how long they will pay you for) differ between policies so, again, make sure you know what you are covered for. If you have multiple funds, check that you're not paying for too much income protection insurance. For example, if you have this insurance on two different super funds and one pays you 85% of your income if you're unable to work, the other insurance can't make up the shortfall.

Benefits of insurance in super

- Less impact on your cashflow.
- Usually easier to get in terms of health checks and disclosures.
- Often cheaper than standalone policies as it's a group policy with all the other members. Think 'buy in bulk' discounts.

Disadvantages of insurance in super

- As it's a group policy, what's covered in the policy can change at any time. For example, the insurer may choose to no longer cover a specific condition that they previously did, or they may change the payment terms.
- There are usually less 'bells and whistles' offered in superannuation policies than you could get if you had a policy in your own name outside superannuation, meaning that the amount of cover you can get is less.
- Not only do you need to meet the insurance conditions to claim, but you need to meet a condition of release to access the payout. What this means is an extra hoop to jump through at claim time, which you wouldn't have if the policy was in your own name.
- Tax treatment differs, for example a TPD payout on a policy you own outside of superannuation is tax-free. For a TPD payout within superannuation, a portion of it will be taxable.

Like anything it's important you understand the pros and cons and weigh up what is best for you as everyone's situation is different.

Our best advice is to get advice! It's also why we include insurance reviews with our membership at LFC, because it can be a bit of a minefield.

Estate planning and your superannuation

Did you know that if you don't nominate an eligible beneficiary on your super fund (who you want your super to go to), the trustee of the superannuation fund has discretion over who your benefits are paid to when you pass away?

If you don't have a nomination in place, or the beneficiary you have nominated doesn't meet the legal definition of dependent, the trustee will need to step in. They have a legal obligation to pay a death benefit to your dependents. It gets tricky if the trustee recognises a wider range of dependents than you would have liked, such as a separated spouse or estranged family members. It can become a drawn-out, messy process.

Your super fund will confirm what options you have in terms of nominating a beneficiary. These generally include a binding beneficiary and a non-binding beneficiary. Think of binding as instructions the trustee must follow. Whereas non-binding is more like a suggestion that you would like them to consider, but they don't have to. The options may also have an expiry where you need to update your beneficiary nomination after a certain period, like three years.

Make sure you have a valid nomination on your super fund that reflects your wishes. If you're not sure who you should, or can, nominate get advice from an estate-planning solicitor. You can literally just log into your super fund to do this.

That's a wrap!

Ladies we need to give a shit about super. We are living longer (on average five years) and retiring with less (currently 47% less) and there is still the pay gap for men and women doing the same job, which isn't going anywhere fast, plus women take on average five years out of the workforce to work part-time or casually. Overall we need our money to last longer.

Your superannuation is money that you exchanged your time and energy for. If you had a car worth over $50,000 you would know where it was at all times. Think of your super like that, but better! It will support your retirement. We see women who had good jobs retiring into poverty because they thought it would all 'just work out'. We don't want that for you, so instead of popping on a Netflix ep, take ten minutes to take one action that will help your future. Trust me, your future self will love you for it!

To action with your gal pals

- [ ] Check how your balance is tracking for your age against the ASFA super balance.
- [ ] Make sure your super is being paid if you're an employee, or your own contributions have been going in.
- [ ] Play around with the Moneysmart retirement calculator and see if you're contributing enough.
- [ ] Nominate the person you want as a beneficiary or check that your nomination hasn't expired.
- [ ] Review whether you're comfortable with the investment allocation, how it's performing, and the fee you are paying.
- [ ] Decide whether you want to consolidate your super funds, and always check what insurances you might be losing.
- [ ] Understand what insurance you currently have and consider if you have too much or not enough.

CHAPTER 8

Investing 101

The first time I tried to invest it reminded me of the time (the one and only time) I went to the free weights section of my gym.

It was intimidating, I didn't know what the hell I was meant to be doing with the weights and there was zero signage. I really didn't know if I was doing it right and didn't want to cause myself long-term damage, plus I was like, 'Where are all my ladies?' I lasted five minutes and then scooted off to yoga. Investing can feel the same. There is jargon for days, it's very male-dominated, it can be intimidating and it's really easy to feel like you don't belong.

But the more I have learnt about investing over the years, the more I feel like I've been let in on the 'secret of how to invest'. And guess what? It's really simple once you have the basics down pat – and you bet that we are going to show you how!

Sometimes finance people make it really complicated and complex, so we are just going to give you the starting steps. When it comes to the actual 'buying part' of share investing, if you can shop online (which, c'mon, we definitely can!) then you can invest online. It's a very simple process.

First, I want to squish some investing myths I hear all the time which might be holding you back from getting started.

Myth 1 Investing is like gambling

Yes, there is an element of risk but it's very different from putting all your money on red! There are many ways you can reduce that risk by diversifying (more on this later), doing research, and holding for the long term where history shows the market goes up. That's very different from putting all your money on horse number eight and crossing your fingers.

Myth 2 But my mate Craig lost all his money investing

I went on a date with a 'Craig' and it goes something like this:

> Me [a few drinks in]: So tell me, Craig, do you invest? [Yes, I do ask this question. I know, I can't understand why I'm still single.]
>
> Craig: No, I invested once and lost all my money. Never again.
>
> Me: Did you happen to invest your money all into one company?
>
> Craig: Yep.
>
> Me: Did you find out about the original company from a 'mate' who worked in finance?
>
> Craig: Yes, but it was my mate's mate.

Okay, ladies, you're savvy, you get what's going on here – investing all your money into one company is risky as hell so we will show you how to spread your money across hundreds, even thousands, of companies in one move (and no, you don't have to pick each company – it's much easier than that, phew).

Myth 3 Now is a bad time to invest

Not even the top experts know what the market will do for sure. I mean, they can make some really good guesses. That's why we are all about taking a long-term approach to investing, because history shows that the market goes up over time (this is a line you'll hear me say a lot).

Myth 4 You'll have to do a heap of research

Belinda White, creator of the online blog Fierce Girl Finance, said there's a middle ground between being totally clueless and a certified expert. 'You need to approach investing with a basic understanding of risk and reward, but waiting until you're an expert might mean you put it off forever.'

Myth 5 You have to be Richie Rich

My god I loved that movie, but you can literally start with $1.

Myth squished.

Myth 6 Investing is for men

Jokes, no one thinks this, I just put that one in there for a LOL.

Also, studies show women make better investors than men, but it's not a competition. Although, if it was, we would win!

Myth 7 I'm too old to invest

As you get older you might take less risk, but you're never too old. Even in your sixties you still have over 20 years for compounding to do its thing!

Myth 8 I won't be able to get my money back for ages

Wrong! Most broker platforms allow you to withdraw your money once you have sold within one to three working days. That's the great thing about investing in the stock market versus property, it's a lot more liquid (you can turn it into cash easily). But, remember, we want our money to be invested for the long term (this will be etched into your brain by the end of this chapter)!

What is the stock market exactly?

Think of it like any market but instead of selling fruit, veg and random antiques, it's a place where companies like Woolworths, Apple, McDonald's or Tesla sell small parts of themselves so they can raise money to create new products, build new stores and factories and keep innovating and expanding. When you buy a small part in these publicly listed companies, you become a shareholder (because you bought a share in that company). Let's say you invested in a large tech company and bought some of their shares. You would become a very, very, very tiny shareholder – a part owner – in that company. When the company makes money, you get some of that profit too.

The amount it costs you to buy a share (the share price) is determined by a few things, the main one being supply and demand (how many people want to buy it and how many people want to sell it).

Over the last 100 years the Australian (and global) stock market has always gone up, but it's not a smooth line, it's more like this:

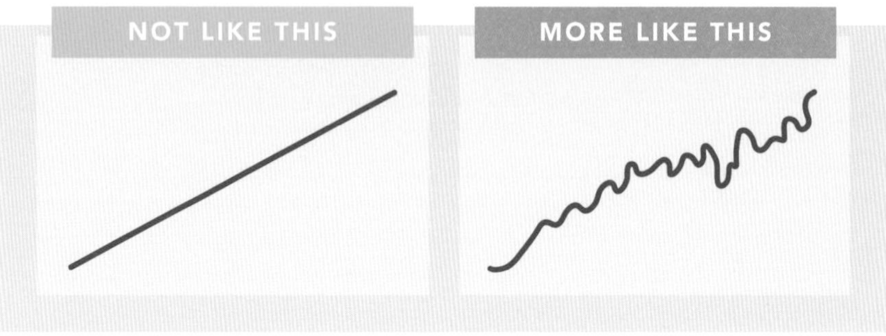

Will the stock market always go up? Well, the markets have continued to rise, even after wars, pandemics and global crises. If you think that we as humans are going to keep innovating, creating, buying, selling and building new products and services then you might want to think about getting involved.

AUSTRALIAN SHARES HAVE CLIMBED A WALL OF WORRY

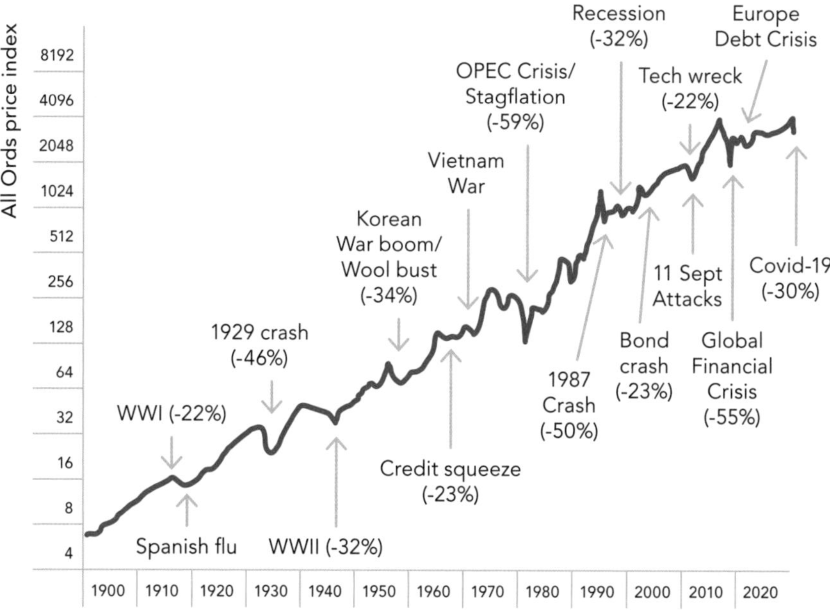

Major share market falls shown in brackets.
Graph source: ASX, AMP Capital

Active vs passive investing

There's a big misconception that investing is about picking stocks, like our mate Craig thought. But if you're not surprisingly up-to-date with which Japanese banks to buy or which American pharmaceutical companies are doing the best, don't worry – we have a much easier way. And no, it's not listening to Uncle Terry's stock tips at the family barbeque.

Personally, I don't have enough experience to pick winning stocks, and the chances are you don't either. Even the people who get paid to pick stock struggle to outperform the market. The fund manager uses their expertise, knowledge and insight to try to pick the right shares and time the market, but many can get it wrong. In 2020, 81% of Aussie fund managers failed to outperform the indexes over ten years. And in the US 92% failed to beat the S&P 500 (top 500 companies in the US) over ten years.

Jargon schmargon

Financial Planner: Professional who gives advice about managing your money to reach your financial goals.

Stockbroker: Licensed professionals who buy and sells stocks on behalf of their clients.

Fund Manager: The people in charge of managing both the day-to-day and long-term operations of a fund.

With active investing, yourself, a stockbroker or a fund manager choose the stocks to invest in. When you invest through a fund manager, you essentially hand over your money and put up all the risk, the fund managers put in no money and no risk. If they lose, you still have to pay them and if you win, you still pay them.

Orlando the cat and a monkey from Princeton have picked better than the 'experts'. What am I talking about? In Princeton in 1973, Professor Malkiel believed that a blindfolded monkey throwing darts at a newspaper's financial pages could pick a better portfolio than the experts. The result? The monkey did much better. They did a similar experiment with a cat called Orlando and the same thing happened. They both outperformed the experts. Don't get us wrong, there are some really good fund managers but the chances of finding them can be low.

Active investing can also get really expensive with fees anywhere from 1% to 3%. So what is the alternative?

If active investing is a hands-on approach then passive investing is a hands-off approach; it's about spreading money across big parts of the stock market. It's not as sexy or exciting but history shows that buying and holding stocks offers the best returns over the long term. As I always say, 'If passive investing was an ice-cream flavour it would be vanilla.'

Passive investing is a good option for people who don't like to pay fees (which I imagine is a lot of people)! It also appeals to people who are time-poor and don't have time to do research – also me.

Before we get into the juicy stuff of how you buy investments, we need to check these three things:

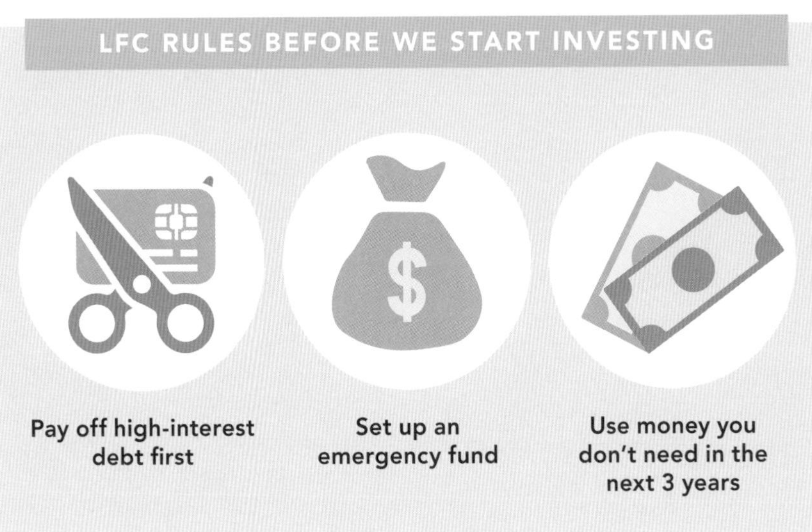

1 Ditch the debt

Picture a gal walking up an escalator the wrong way. That's what you're doing if you have bad debt and start investing. You need to get rid of any bad debt or debt with a high interest rate.

We mean: credit cards, personal loans, BNPLs.

We don't mean: student loans and mortgages.

If you make a 9.3% return on your investments (which was the average return of the ASX 200 over the last ten years) and you're paying off a credit card with an 18% interest rate – you're still going backwards. So ditch the debt first!

2 Set up your OMG fund

There was a whole chapter on this bad boy (Chapter 4) and I know you're a money savvv-ay lady so you have already set this up. But let's say you need money asap (the car broke down) and all your money is invested. If the stock market is down (which happens), by taking out that money you are locking in that loss. Remember the stock market is like a rollercoaster. That's why when people took their $10k of superannuation out during Covid they were locking in their losses as the market recovered only a few months later.

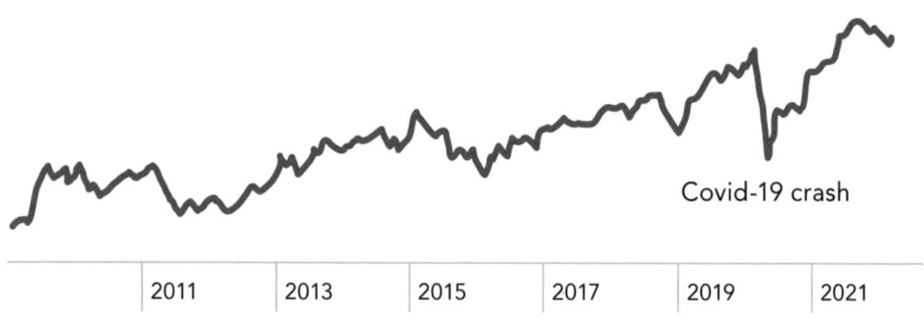

3 Only ever use money you don't need in the next three to five years

If you wanted to buy a house in the next year or two you wouldn't want to invest because if the market took a downturn and didn't recover for a while, then you would either have to wait to buy the house or take out your money and risk a loss. If your goal is to retire in ten years or save for an apartment in five years, you may consider investing that money because you have time for the market to recover.

7 simple concepts for investing!

1 Start now!

Let's say you had $10,000 in 2000, what would it be worth if you had:

1. Left it under your mattress
2. Left it in cash at a bank in a savings account
3. Invested it in the share market?

Here's what you would have earned:

1. Under the mattress = $10,000 (although less due to inflation – more on that later)
2. Cash at a bank = $23,042
3. Invested it = $60,677*

*Based on Australian shares average return of 8.5%

Source: Vanguard Digital Index Chart

(On all investments you'll see some text which says. 'Past performance is not an indication of future returns.' This means just because an investment had an 8.5% return one year doesn't mean it will get that same return next year.)

Sweet compounding returns

Compounding returns is the most important concept in investing, so I want to make sure you really understand it.

If I said, 'What would you rather receive: 1 cent that doubles every day for 30 days or $10,000 every day for a month (30 days)?'

You might think, 'Jeez, Molly, I'll take the $10,000 a day please', which would mean after 30 days you would have $300,000.

Had you chosen the cent that doubled every day you would be kicking back with over $5 million big ones (or $5,368,709 to be exact). Crazy, right?

How is this so?

The power of compounding.

Compound interest is often referred to as 'interest on the interest', or when your money is making money. Because the interest you earn on the original money becomes bigger than the money you had there in the first place.

Confused? Let's look at an example of myself and my twin sister Rhianna.

Rhi and I both decide to invest. I start investing at 30 years old and Rhi starts investing at 40 years old. We both invest $500 a month every year until we retire at 65 years old.

At retirement, I have invested a total amount of $210,000 and Rhianna has invested $150,000 – a $60,000 difference.

But come retirement, thanks to compounding interest, my total balance is over $1 million ($1,033,901) and Rhianna's is just over $400,000 ($438,636). That's over $500,000 difference because I started investing ten years earlier! Danielle Ecuyer, founder of share investing education website Shareplicity, says, 'Time is the secret ingredient for share investors!'

Let's look at it from another angle. Let's say you were earning 10% interest annually on $100.

Year 1: $100 + 10% = $110 (+$10)

Year 2: $110 + 10% = $121 (+$11) (since this year you're starting with $110 rather than $100)

Year 3: $121 + 10% = $133 (+$12)

Year 4: $133 + 10% = $146 (+$13)

Year 5: $146 + 10% = $161 (+$15)

And so on and so on and you get this snowball effect where the interest eventually becomes bigger than the original (principal) amount.

2 Inflation is eating your money

For those who remember, McDonald's used to have a soft-serve called the 30-cent cone. That 30-cent cone now costs 70 cents, and that is inflation. The end. Mic drop!

Inflation is when the cost of living goes up. If you went to Coles and bought a trolley of groceries for $100, then next year you popped into Coles and bought exactly the same items but it cost $106, that's inflation. It reduces our purchasing power.

At the time of writing this book, the Consumer Price Index (CPI), which is how economists measure inflation, is at 6.1%, the highest it's been since 1990. The RBA likes inflation to be around 2–3%. There are a number of reasons why inflation is high, including supply and demand, Covid recovery, climate change and war to name a few.

Inflation means while your money is sitting in the bank making a very small amount of interest, it is going backwards in real value. This is another reason why you might want to think about investing.

3 Asset classes

To explain asset classes in simple terms we are borrowing this analogy from Emma Kirk, who works with an Australian-based investment firm called Magellan. This is how she explained the different asset classes at an event of ours that she spoke at:

When you're trying to get fit, you have some different choices about what type of exercise you want to do – the same goes for investing. You have a choice as to what you are comfortable investing in and what outcomes will arise based on those decisions.

When you invest you have a choice of asset classes, broadly:

- **Cash:** This is where you can invest in things like a term deposit and get interest on your money. Your money is guaranteed but in today's environment, you're not likely to get a lot of return.
  Return = interest earned
- **Fixed income:** This is where you are investing in bonds issued by a government or a company. You lend them money and they pay you back a set rate of interest over a period of time. The value of the amount you lend them can go up or down depending on what interest rates are doing.
  Return = yield (similar to interest)
- **Property:** Lots of people like property because they can

understand it and they can see it. You invest in a property or a combination of properties and your return is based on the rent or income that you receive and the increase in the value of that property (which can go up or down). Property can involve retail, commercial or industrial assets like airports, supermarkets and work buildings, or Australian real estate investment trusts (A-REITs) that you can buy on the stock market.

Return = rent or capital gains/losses

- **Australian shares:** These are where you can own a slice of some Australian companies listed on the Australian Securities Exchange (ASX). Returns are made up of dividends, or if the company's share price goes up over time then your investment is worth more.

  Return = capital gains/losses + dividends

- **Global shares:** Instead of being listed on the ASX, these are listed on a securities exchange overseas, like the New York Stock Exchange (NYSE) or London Stock Exchange (LSE). The returns you receive from global companies are more likely to be in the form of an increase in share price (or capital growth) than dividends.

  Return = capital gains/losses + dividends

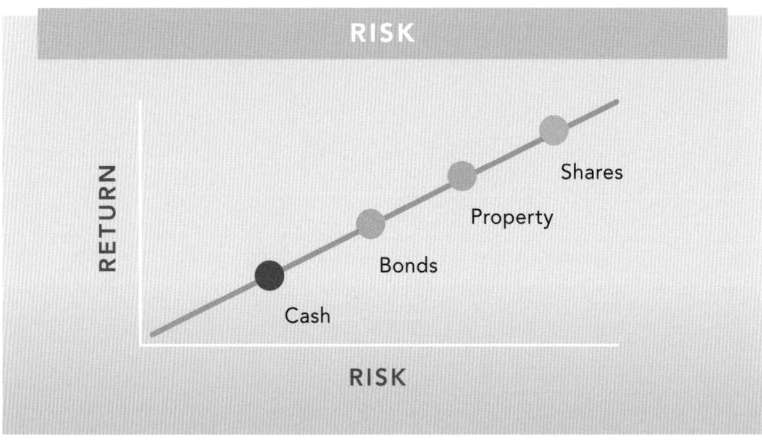

4 Your risk level

Our risk profile (how much risk we are comfortable taking) will differ from person to person. For example, I have a higher 'risk tolerance' than my twin sister Rhi. I know that the markets will go up and down and I'm comfortable with that. My sister wants to buy a house in the next few years so she isn't looking to take too many risks.

I like to think of risk profiles as shoe types:

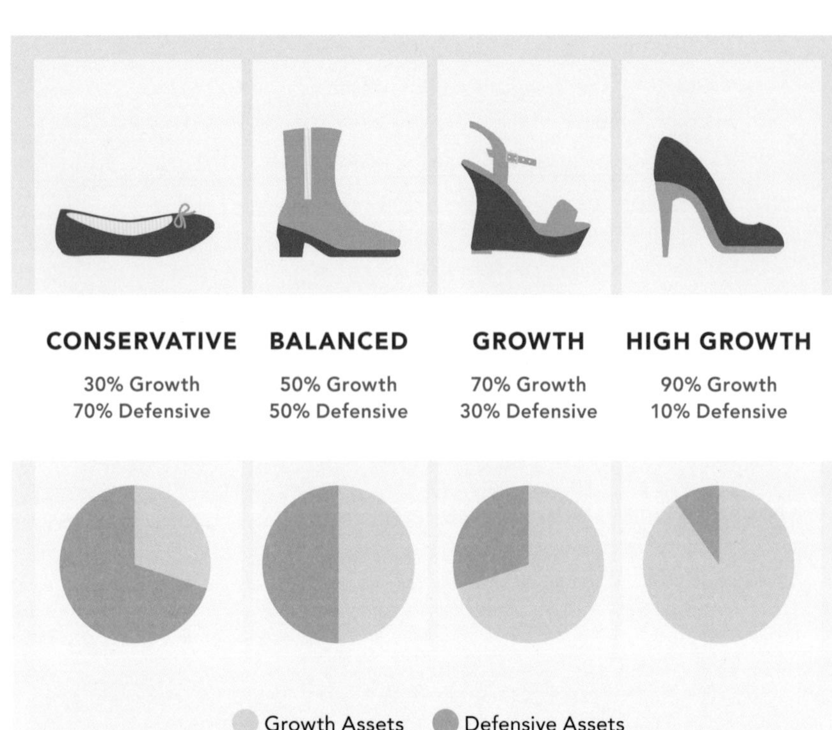

Note: Don't just take an investment's name at face value. For example, a 'balanced' fund may actually have up to 80% in growth assets and not be a typical balanced fund at all. Check out investments via the provider's website to see what the growth and defensive split is.

This is the ASIC Moneysmart's risk profile so you can work out what yours is.

Your comfort and experience	Your investment time frame		
	Short term (1–3 years)	Medium term (4–6 years)	Long term (7+ years)
Relaxed, confident, experienced	Cash	Balanced	Growth
Somewhere in the middle	Cash	Conservative	Balanced
Nervous, anxious, inexperienced	Cash	Conservative	Conservative

The asset classes also align with risk areas. Cash and bonds are defensive assets as they provide a steady, stable income stream that generally has lower investment risk, but also the potential for lower returns over the longer term. Property and shares are growth assets as they have the potential for higher investment returns over the longer term, but they also tend to have higher investment risk (they are more volatile) short term. That's why we see people who are younger investing in more growth assets compared to those close to retirement who want to defend what they have!

5 Spread the risk

If you have all your money in one or two companies and they don't go well, you might lose lots of money. Like Craig. If you spread your investments across lots of different industries across different countries and assets classes you can protect yourself from ups and downs.

People always use the example of Blockbuster Video (if you're like, 'Who are they?' that's our point exactly).

Blockbuster was one of the biggest video rental companies in America. Netflix wanted Blockbuster to buy them for a mere $50 million but Blockbuster refused. Fast forward more than ten years and Netflix is now worth $176.07 billion while Blockbuster filed for bankruptcy in 2010. If you had 100% of your money in Blockbuster you would have lost it all.

Not keen on picking your own stock in case you pick a bad one like Craig? Index funds might be an option for you to look at.

6 Don't want to pick stocks?

Remember how we told you about the monkey who picked better stocks than the finance 'experts' and that only 19% of fund managers could outperform the market? If you don't want to pick stocks and pay big fees to someone who might (but might not) beat the market, how do you invest in the stock market as a whole? The good news is you don't have to buy one of everything – there's a product that does that for you! They are called index funds or exchange-traded funds (ETFs).

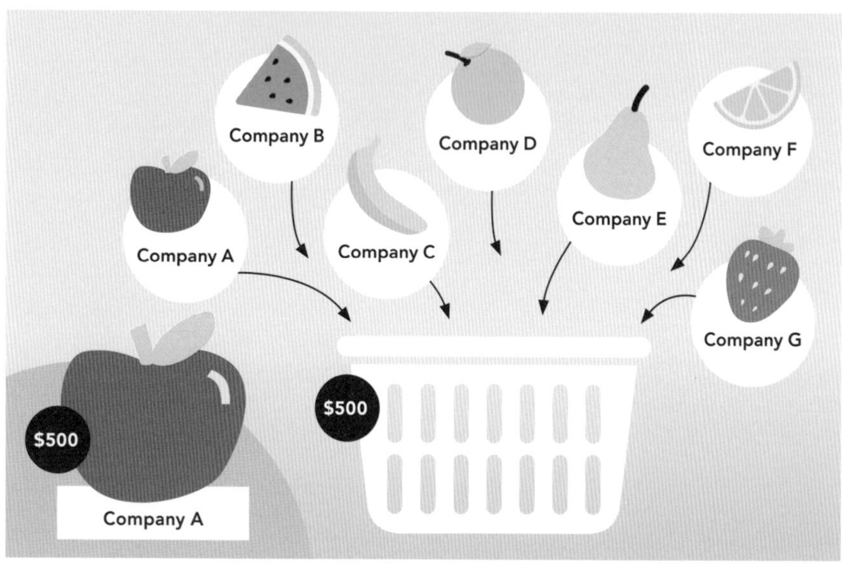

I like to think of ETFs like a basket of fruit! You're not just getting a basket of apples, you're getting a basket of mixed fruit – cherries, blueberries, starfruit (whatever they are), mangoes … you get the gist. With ETFs you're not just getting one company, you're getting a mix of companies already prepared for you.

Let's pretend that a basket of fruit represents the ASX 200 (the top 200 companies in Australia). You would get some Woolworths, Domino's, CommBank, NAB, BHP, CSL, plus 194 other companies!

Where to buy

Remember our fruit basket analogy? When you go to market there are stalls (brokers) where you buy your fruit. You can buy individual pieces of fruit (stocks and shares) or mixed baskets of fruit (index funds and ETFs). In Australia, we have lots of online brokers (stalls) but not all stalls are the same.

Another way I like to put this is: imagine if you wanted to buy a L'Oreal classic red lipstick. There are lots of places I can buy that lipstick from – I can buy it from Adore Beauty, Priceline, Chemist Warehouse, Sephora – but I am still buying the exact same lipstick. It's the same with stocks, you can buy the same one from a number of different places.

Here's a list of some common brokers in Australia:

Traditional places

- nabtrade
- CommSec
- Westpac

New kids on the block

- Superhero
- Pearler
- SelfWealth

- Sharesies
- eToro
- Stake

Some of them will have different brokerage (the fee for buying and selling shares) but most will be between $5 and $20. And some will have an initial minimum investment amount of up to $500.

How do you know which investment to choose?

In Australia, there are over 260 different ETFs on the Australian Stock Exchange.

Some types of ETFs you can get include:

- **Australian equities (Aussie companies):** like the top companies in Australia.
- **Global equities:** the top 500 companies in America, companies based in Asia, top non-financial 100 companies such as Google, Facebook, Amazon, Netflix, Apple, Tesla.
- **Commodities:** such as gold, silver, oil.
- **Thematic:** a fund that offers the opportunity to invest based on a particular theme, such as climate change, artificial intelligence, infrastructure … even weed ETFs.
- **Property:** this is a way to get into property without worrying about a mortgage.
- **Ethical:** Ethical investing is a way to hold companies accountable for the environmental, social and ethical consequences of their actions and you can choose ETFs that meet certain sustainable criteria. Different investment companies will have different criteria about what is ethical and sustainable to them so it's important to always look at what they are investing in and if it aligns with your values.
- **Dividend:** ETFs that pay you dividends.

And loads more.

But who is supplying the mixed baskets of fruit to the fruit stalls? These are investment companies. Some big ones are Vanguard, BlackRock and BetaShares but there are many more.

Right now you're thinking, 'OMG, there are sooo many ETFs, how do I know which one to pick?' Well, that's what we can't tell you, unfortunately, but we can say: always invest in what you understand, and do your research.

What are the differences between ETFs and index funds?

Much like Kourtney and Khloé Kardashian, they are easy to confuse because they are really similar. The main difference is how you buy them. You can buy ETFs through a broker (fruit stall) on the ASX but to buy an index fund you have to go to the fruit supplier (the investment company).

 Keep costs low

Generally in life, the more you pay for something the better it is – like fancy hotels, the black plates at sushi restaurants, that really expensive Aesop hand cream. With fees, it is different. Fees can really eat into any profits you make – just like we spoke about compounding returns, your fees also compound.

Let's look at three friends: Amy, Kat and Natalie.

All friends start by investing $5000 and then commit to investing $100 every month for 30 years. They all get an average return of 7%.

Amy chooses a passive investment with a low fee of 0.10%

Kat chooses an active fund with 1% fee

Natalie gets an advisor to manage her money which has a 2% fee plus an advisor fee of 1%.

After 30 years they have the following:

Amy Fund balance: $151,621
Fees paid: $3,386

Kat Fund balance: $124,658
Fees paid: $30,348

Natalie Fund balance: $82,341
Fees paid: $72,665

How to make money through investing

There are two main ways to make money through investing.

1. **Capital Growth.** This is your investment increasing in value over time. For example, if you bought 100 shares or ETFs in 2016 for $55 each (a total of $5500) and then you sold them for $323 each (a total of $32,300) you would make a capital gain of $26,800. You would have to pay tax on this capital gain. By holding on to an asset for longer than one year you can potentially get a 50% discount your capital gain – another way the government is encouraging us to invest for the long term!
2. **Dividends.** When the company makes a profit they share some of that profit with you! 🎁 #Yippee!

You can choose to automatically reinvest the dividend or take it in cash.

Not all companies pay a dividend. Some reinvest their profit back into their company to keep growing or give to the owners. Some ETFs will pay dividends.

Let's use an Aussie bank example:

Aussie bank A pays a dividend of $2 per share twice a year. You have 100 shares = $400 per year.

I feel like we have the basics down pat now so it's time to buy!

BUYING SHARES + ETFS

Buying shares and ETFs

There are a few ways you can get started investing. Remember, it's really important to look at your goals and ensure you are only investing money you don't need for the short term.

The process of buying ETFs/shares is similar to that of buying a dress on eBay.

1. Sign up to a broker account (they will want to know your basic details, like name, TFN, address, email etc.).
2. Once you're in, take a look around, find the investment you want to buy by looking up the ticker code (usually three–four letters).
3. Decide how much you want to invest and fill out the order pad.

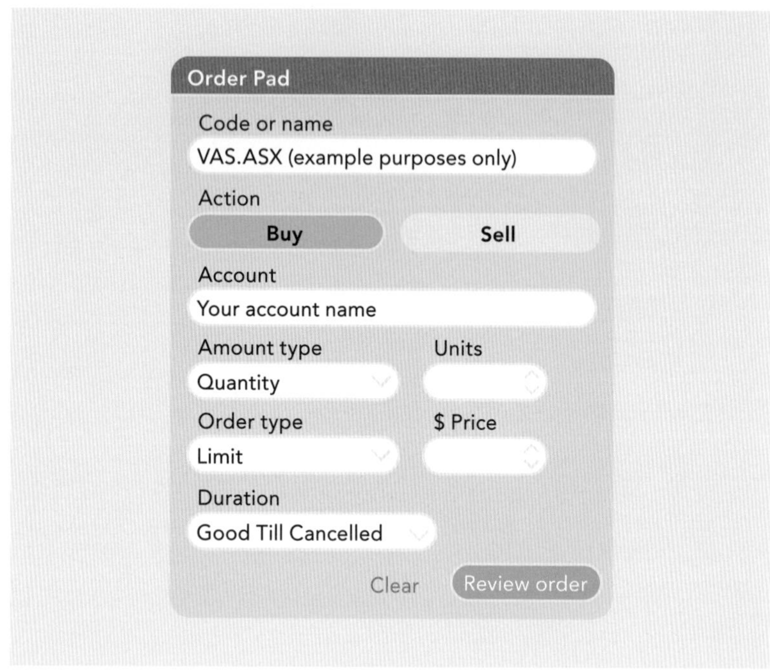

4. Place the order. You will have two options: Market Price or Limit Price (this just means do you want to pay the market price or put a limit on the price – like buy now on eBay or bid). And then you can choose how many investments you want to buy or by how much money you have to spend.
5. Deposit the money (sometimes they make you do this earlier) and hit review order, then confirm.
6. You'll be notified when the confirmation comes through, which might be immediately or a little bit later on if the market is closed – the ASX is open from 10am to 4pm (NSW).
7. Later, once it has gone through, you'll get a letter in the mail which has your HIN number (like a bank identification number but for your investments) and you can login to your share registry and update your details.

Share registries

A 'share registry' is a company that manages the registry of shareholders for that company. The registry has the following responsibilities:

🤑 Recording changes in share ownership

🤑 Issuing shareholding statements and communications

🤑 Managing dividend payments, bonuses and rights issues.

When you purchase shares or ETFs you will need to visit the website of the share registry and create an account in order to instruct them on how to treat your dividends. Brokers don't manage this. Some big share registries in Australia include Computershare, Link Market Services and Automic Group and BoardRoom Pty Limited.

Once logged in, you can edit your details, your communication preferences (from post to email) and whether you want your dividends to be reinvested into the company.

Micro investing

These apps are a good starting place for beginners and are about making small investments from everyday transactions. For example, a cappuccino at $4.50 will be rounded up to $5 and the 50 cents would then be invested.

Aussie micro-investing apps include:

- CommSec Pocket
- Raiz
- Spaceship
- Bamboo (crypto only)

Robo-advisors

These are investment management companies that rely on computers rather than human financial advisors. They will put you into an investment based on your data, goals, risk and time frame.

Aussie companies offering this include:

- Stockspot
- Spaceship
- Six Park

Jargon schmargon

ASX 200 – the 200 largest Australian-listed companies

All Ordinaries (All Ords) – the 500 largest Australian-listed companies

S&P 500 – the 500 largest US-listed companies (by market cap)

Nasdaq – the 100 largest non-financial companies (e.g. Facebook, Google, Amazon)

FTSE 100 – the 100 largest companies on the London Stock Exchange

Keep your emotions in check

Investing can be a rollercoaster for your emotions: 'I lost $100. I'm ruined, sell, sell, sell!' or 'It's gone up $250, woohoo, I'm rich!' What makes a good investor is the ability to keep your emotions in check. Imagine having freaked out and sold all your investments during Covid, you would have missed out on the great returns that followed very quickly afterwards. Smart investors stick to the plan, they block out the media noise and are in for the long term.

When should you invest?

Consistency is key when it comes to investing. If you can automate your investments so you're doing it monthly then you will be automatically dollar-cost averaging. Dollar-cost averaging simply involves investing the same amount of money into the market at regular intervals over a long period. Let's say you have $1200 to invest, you might invest $300 one month and purchase ten shares, then the next month the market is down and you can buy 30 shares with that $300 and so on.

Some platforms even let you set this up so money is automatically taken from your account and invested so you don't even have to think about it.

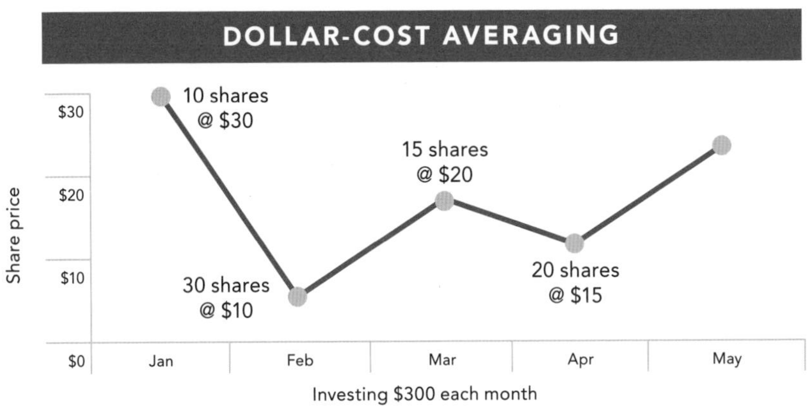

What about crypto?

Tracey Plowman, COO of crypto micro-investing app Bamboo, says you cannot cover off on modern-day finance without talking about cryptocurrency and blockchain technology.

Rising from the ashes of the global financial crisis and the brainchild of an anonymous person or group going by the name of Satoshi Nakamoto, Bitcoin and the many subsequent cryptocurrencies offer a digital peer-to-peer transfer of cash, free from intermediaries such as banks and governments – they're decentralised.

Fast-forward 14 years and things have moved at breakneck speed.

In simple terms, blockchain is a cryptographic technology that uses mathematical code. By design, this reduces any possibility of manipulating the data since it uses complex mathematics to solve a puzzle beyond our comprehension.

Because of the lack of intermediaries, it is cheaper and more efficient than hiring or paying for a third party's services.

Many cryptocurrencies are decentralised networks based on blockchain technology. There are tens of thousands of different crypto coins out there and it's extremely volatile. Billionaire investor Ray Dalio says you should only invest 1%–2% into your crypto. You must be willing to lose what you put in and, like all investing, it should be for the long term.

That's a wrap!

I want to leave you with a story I love. Sylvia Bloom worked as a legal secretary for 67 years at Cleary Gottlieb Steen & Hamilton, a Wall Street law firm. When the boss would buy stock, she would make the purchase for him, and then buy the same stock for herself, but in a smaller amount. She lived very modestly and when she passed away her family were very surprised to find out that she was a multimillionaire. In her will, she donated over $8 million to charities. Investing is not about day trading, or trying to pick stocks and beat the market. History shows that investing in the stock market offers the best returns over the long term. It's way less dramatic than the movies and you don't have to be the wolf of Wall Street. Watch out for fees above 1%, and if you're still confused, as we always say … the best advice is to get advice.

Look at you turning into Mini Miss Buffetts!

To action with your gal pals

- ☐ Check you're ready to invest (you have an OMG fund, no high interest debt, and don't need the money for the next three to five years).
- ☐ Decide whether you want to do active or passive investing (or both).
- ☐ Open a broker account or micro-investing app.
- ☐ Decide what to invest in.
- ☐ Buy your investments and set up an automatic payment.

CHAPTER 9

Talk Nerdy to Me

Tax is like the yearly subscription you pay to the country you live in (childhood is the free version).

There are several different taxes in Australia (GST, CGT, business tax) but this chapter will focus on income tax.

This will be the quickest lesson you will ever get in tax and how to legally pay less (keyword: *legally*).

Let's talk tax

Tax gets a bad rap but it means we have great schools, roads and a healthcare system, and all Aussies are looked after. The goal is to ensure you don't pay more than you need to.

The Australian financial year ends on 30 June. You have from 1 July to 31 October to lodge your tax return for the previous income year. If you use a registered tax agent, you've actually got until 16 May the following year, which gives you (and your accountant) some breathing room.

Your tax return tells the tax office how much you have earned in income, how much you spent on work-related expenses and how much you already paid in tax during the financial year. These amounts will help determine if you still owe money to the ATO or if it needs to give you a refund because you have paid too much.

Who pays tax?

If you earn more than a certain amount (at the time of publishing the amount is $18,200) in a year, from almost any source, including employment, investments or capital gains, you'll have to pay tax. This includes individuals, sole traders and business owners.

Tax rates

Here's where people often become confused. Tax in Australia operates on a sliding scale, meaning there isn't a straightforward percentage formula you can apply to figure out how much tax you will owe.

Take a look at the breakdown of tax rates as it applies in 2022–23:

RESIDENT TAX RATES 2022–23	
Taxable income	**Tax on this income**
0–$18,2000	Nil
$18,201–$45,000	19 cents for each $1 over $18,200
$45,001–$120,000	$5092 plus 32.5 cents for each $1 over $45,000
$120,001–$180,000	$29,467 plus 37 cents for each $1 over $120,000
$180,001 and over	$51,667 plus 45 cents for each $1 over $180,000

The above rates **do not** include the Medicare levy of 2%

(Source: ATO)

Let's use Sarah as an example.

Sarah earns $80,000 per year from her job. She pays zero tax on the first $18,200 of this income. The money she earns between $18,200 and $45,000 is taxed at 19%. This totals $5902.

The money Sarah earns between $45,000 and $80,000 is taxed at a higher rate. She'll be taxed 32.5 cents for every dollar she earns.

How much tax does Sarah pay on an $80,000 salary?

$5092 + 32.5% of each $ over $45,000

80,000 – 45,000 = 35,000

35,000 x 32.5% = $11,375

$5092 + $11,375 = $16,467

Sarah has to pay $16,467 in tax at the end of the financial year.

If Sarah had a big jump in pay and started earning more than $120,000, the money she earns above that amount will be taxed at 37%.

You can see why it is tricky to figure out in your head! An online Australian tax calculator can help you do the sums.

Medicare

Just when you thought you had figured out how much tax you owe ...

We looked at the Medicare levy and the Medicare Levy Surcharge (MLS) in Chapter 6. Most of us will contribute 2% of our taxable income to the Medicare levy each year. If you are single and earn over $90,000, or if you're partnered up and earn $180,000 combined, and you don't have private health insurance, your Medicare surcharge may be an extra 1.5% of your income.

What does this mean? Once you have used a tax calculator to figure out what income tax you owe, remember the Medicare levy will bump the amount up a bit.

Student debt

We covered this in Chapter 5 but if you've been to university and weren't able to pay for the fees upfront, you may have incurred a HECS/HELP debt. Your repayments will come out of your salary once you start earning over a certain amount (at the time of writing, $48,361).

What do you have to declare?

Tax in Australia is based on an honour system. While the government has the power to review your income in detail, it relies on you to keep the tax department up to date about what you earned and how much tax you have paid.

Your income can come from numerous places, not just your work. You may have earned money from a side hustle. You could have received a bonus from your job, claimed Centrelink payments or received income from a tenanted investment property. Then there's the income you make from shares or from your savings accounts.

You can fill out your tax return and declare your various income sources yourself, either on paper or online. The other option is to work with a tax accountant.

Let's get back to Sarah from our earlier example. Her grandmother passed away and she received $20,000. This does not have to be declared as income. If she puts this money in the bank and earns interest, the interest she earns from the account qualifies as taxable money so she'll have to declare it in her tax return.

What can you claim?

If you spend money for work-related purposes, you can claim that money as 'lost income'. Things like travel (in some circumstances), income protection insurance, home office expenses (within reason) and even the rent you pay (if you run a business from home) can be tax-deductible.

Our good friend Sarah spent $5000 on a course that gave her up-to-date skills related to her current job. She can claim this expense as a tax deduction. Note that she can't claim the expense if she spent the money on a photography course that she just wanted to do for fun.

Think of it this way: can you prove you needed to spend the money to do your job? If you can justify the expense, you can claim it.

WHAT CAN YOU AND CAN'T YOU CLAIM?	
✓ Can Claim	✗ Can't Claim
☐ Work-related deductions – travel – motor vehicle – education – dry cleaning	☐ Makeup
☐ Investment deductions	☐ Everyday 'work clothes'
☐ Tax advice deductions	☐ Toilet paper
☐ Insurance	☐ Milk, sugar, tea, coffee
☐ Miscellaneous	☐ Luxury stationery
☐ Covid deductions	☐ Business losses
	☐ Child care or homeschooling costs

Looking at the table above, you'll see that you can't claim the cost of regular work clothes unless they are a specific uniform. You also can't claim for makeup (unless you're an actress or air hostess), skincare products, child care or the cost of homeschooling.

Some claims require evidence. For most categories you can claim up to around $300, after which you'll need to have evidence of the expense.

There are several grey areas when it comes to what you can claim. If, for example, you operate a business from home, you can claim some of the cost of your rent but not necessarily your mortgage. The amount you can claim is based on the percentage of your home you use for work. The same may apply to your home internet or phone bill – you can't always claim every dollar but some of the cost can be work-related. There are online calculators to help you work out your costs. If you're confused, it can help to speak with an accountant (and the cost is tax-deductible).

Just remember that the ATO can check your tax return at any time (even years later) and make you pay the savings back, with interest and penalties.

How to legally pay less tax

There are ways to 'play the game' without breaking the rules. For example, making voluntary contributions to your superannuation is tax-deductible (up to a point). It's true that you can't spend it immediately but it still means less of your income goes to the tax office.

You may have expenses coming up that are work-related and unavoidable. If you pay them in full before the end of the financial year, your income drops and you pay less tax.

As an employee, you may be able to explore the option of a novated lease on your vehicle. This means that your car payments are taken out as part of your salary before you get paid. Again, the result is less tax owed at the end of the year.

Do I have to pay tax on my investments?

There's a myth here where everyone seems to think you pay 50% tax! However, there is a capital gains tax (CGT) discount of 50% for Australian individuals who own an asset for 12 months or more. This means you pay tax on only half the net capital gain on that asset.

For example, Stacey is an Aussie resident and buys shares. She owns these for 15 months and makes a profit of $10,000. Stacey is entitled to the 50% CGT discount for the shares and will declare a capital gain of $5000 on her tax return.

Some assets are exempt from CGT, such as your home. Helen Francis, Principal Accountant at TY Francis, says, 'I'm constantly bemused by how much time people can waste focused on how they can reduce their tax bill. If they spent half as much time focusing on how they could increase their tax bill, I guarantee they'd be receiving their tax bills with a smile on their face!'

How do I submit my tax return?

You can submit your tax return using the myGov portal or you can see a tax accountant. They'll ask you questions, ask for evidence of your income and lodge your tax return for you. If you earn wages as an employee, submitting your tax return through an accountant should cost between $100 and $200. When you add a lot of moving parts, for example, due to investments and separate sources of income, you're likely to pay a bit more. The benefit is that you'll probably end up adding several hundred dollars (or more) to your refund.

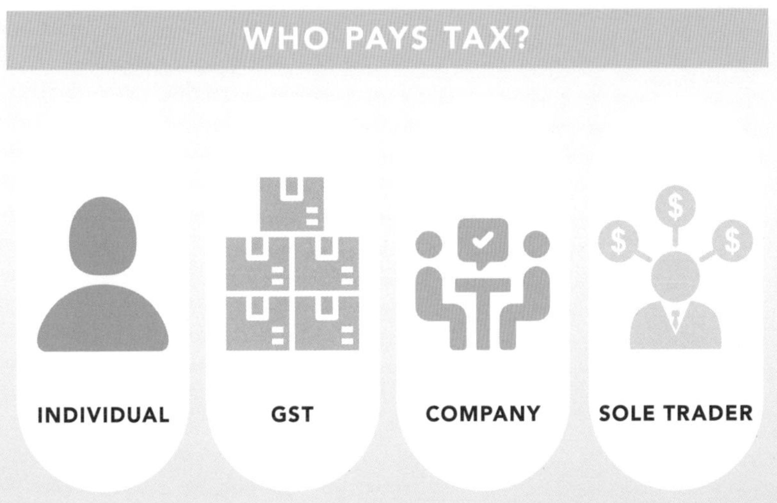

REMEMBER TO CLAIM THESE TAX DEDUCTIONS

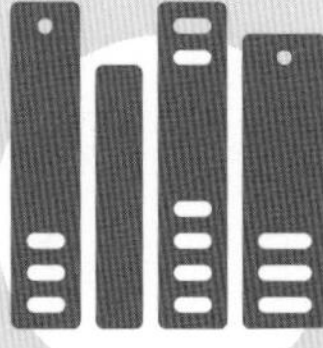

Self-education/ course expenses

Working from home expenses

Insurance

% of work-related car expenses plus travel

% of work-related phone and internet usage

Work-related laundry expenses

Donations

Accountant or tax agent fees for assisting with your tax return

That's a wrap!

Katie Bryan, Founder and CEO of Australia-wide accounting firm Propeller Advisory, says the biggest mistakes she sees people making on their tax returns are not understanding which expenses you can claim, so missing out on deductions that you are entitled to, and not keeping adequate records – there are some great apps available for this including the ATO app, which has a section called myDeductions.

Tax can seem complicated but the ATO has made it very easy for us to submit our returns online. Remember, if you need, reach out to an accountant or join one of the Ladies Finance Club's sessions on tax.

To action with your gal pals

- Find out what tax bracket you are in.
- Find out if you still have a HECS/HELP debt and if it's being taken out of your pay.
- Log on to ATO and ensure you don't have any outstanding tax returns due.
- Work out whether you're better off getting hospital cover or paying the Medicare surcharge levy.

CHAPTER 10

Home and a Loan

It's the Aussie dream to own your own home but with house prices going crazy, and when you need a small mortgage to afford your daily coffee, how can you get on the property ladder? In this chapter we'll help you step onto the ladder, supercharge your deposit and take you from renter to homeowner.

Step 1 Believe you can

I was walking around a nice suburb with a girlfriend and we walked past a pretty white house. 'I'll never be able to afford a house on my own,' my friend said. 'I am not even gonna bother.' She earned $100,000 per year and she was already taking herself out of the game. I knew she could save up for a deposit but maybe she needed to be a bit more 'entrepreneurial' in how she went about it.

Did she know you now only have to cough up between 2% to 10% of a house deposit with some government schemes? Had she thought about rentvesting? Could her parents be a guarantor?

If you really want something you can find ways to make it happen.

That's why step one needs to be actually believing this is possible for yourself.

Step 2 Save up a deposit

If buying property is a goal of yours, open up a fee-free account and label it 'Dream Home fund'. When you get paid, set up an automatic direct debit so money goes straight into this fund. You have to start somewhere so it may as well be with your first dollar.

Not sure how much you should be saving for a deposit? Do some research and get a general understanding of how much prices are where you want to buy – ideally, you want to aim for 20% of the total deposit but there are ways around that – cue Lenders' Mortgage Insurance (LMI). Unlike most insurances, this isn't insuring you, it's insurance for the bank in case you default on your loan repayments. A smaller deposit means a bigger loan and you will also have to pay more for LMI. Generally, you have to pay LMI if you borrow more than 80% of your home's value; this means you can then borrow up to 95% of the deposit.

Deposit required

DEPOSIT NEEDED	5%	10%	20%
$500k home	$25k	$50k	$100k
$800k home	$40k	$80k	$160k
$1 million home	$50k	$100k	$200k
$1.5 million home	$75k	$150k	$300k

Other costs (estimated only)

Purchase price	20% of sale price
Stamp duty	This can vary by state and house price (often $0 for first-home buyers)
Conveyancing and legal fees	$1500–1800
Building and pest inspection	$600
Mortgage registration fee	$187 (differs by state)
Transfer fee (titles)	$35 for every $10,000 over $180,000 (differs by state)
Loan application fee (costs associated with setting up a loan with a lender)	$600
LMI (with only 10% deposit)	Will depend on property
Council and water rates	$500

Step 3 Organise your A-team

You are not meant to know everything about buying a property so you want to get people around you who do. Who is in your A-team?

MORTGAGE BROKER	Mortgage brokers are like free personal shoppers. They know the shops (loan providers and banks) well and who's going to fit your shape (circumstances). They go out and find you some really good options (loans). And you don't have to pay them – the loan provider does that! Mortgage brokers are generally the first people you would reach out to as you need to know how much you can actually borrow – or, if we're getting all formal, 'what your lending capability is'. A broker will look at you as a whole picture – your deposit, your spending behaviours, employment situation – and find a loan provider who will be best for you. Leading Sydney mortgage broker Kathy Euers from INK Wealth says, 'If you walk into a bank, you're limited. You could be a square peg trying to fit into a round hole with that particular bank's policy. If you use a broker they will have about 30 different lenders and hundreds of different loan options that they can source for you.'
ACCOUNTANT	If you are self-employed you might need to work closely with your accountant to make sure that your financials are stacking up.
REAL ESTATE AGENTS	Time to befriend your local real estate agent! A real estate agent gets paid by the person selling the house (the vendor) – they usually get a commission of the sale which can range from 1% to 3% depending on certain factors.
BUYER'S AGENT (OPTIONAL)	A buyer's agent specialises in searching for, evaluating and negotiating properties on your behalf. Their fees can be a flat fee or commission-based.

PEST INSPECTOR AND BUILDING INSPECTOR	A building inspector will make sure the house has been built correctly and look for any significant defects or problems such as rising damp, movement in the walls or a dodgy roof. The pest inspection will check for termites and other creepy crawlies.
CONVEYANCER	A conveyancer or conveyancing solicitor will help with the settlement and title transfer process by ensuring that the seller is meeting all their legal obligations and that your rights are protected during this transaction. They will complete the preparation, execution and lodgement of various legal documents to enable a swift and legal sale.

Fast-track your deposit

Government assistance

Mortgage Choice advisor Emma Stephens says it's definitely worth looking at what schemes are available. 'To help the first-time home buyers get on the property ladder, the government offers different support schemes that are really beneficial to women.' You can check out what you're eligible for here: nhfic.gov.au/eligibility/.

- **First Home Owner Grant** helps those who want somewhere to live, not people looking to invest in property. Check your eligibility in your state here: firsthome.gov.au/.
- **The First Home Loan Deposit Scheme** is a federal government initiative which allows you to purchase a home with a 5% deposit and avoid paying LMI. There are only 10,000 spots and you have to meet certain criteria.
- **First Home Super Saver Scheme** can be used by first-home buyers to save money inside their super fund to help buy their first home.

- **Family Home Guarantee** is for single parents with at least one dependent. You can buy your own home with a deposit as small as 2% and with no LMI.
- **Stamp duty relief** is offered by almost all states to some first-home buyers. Check your state's stamp duty website.

Rentvesting

Buyer's agent Julie Crockett from Australian Property Investment Solutions describes 'rentvesting' as renting where you want to live, maybe by the beach, and starting your property journey as an investor. If you live in Sydney or Melbourne, buying an investment property in another capital city usually comes at a much lower price tag and gets you into the market sooner. You won't get the first-home buyer grant or other government incentives when you buy an investment property but you can claim the expenses on the rental property on your tax. In the same time it may have taken you to save that huge deposit to buy a 'home' you may have two investment properties in your pocket. You can then use the capital growth in your investment properties to get you into your forever home down the track.

Financial gifting

For families with the financial means to do so, gifting part of the deposit may be an option. When you lodge a loan, you fill out a letter saying how much your parents or other family are agreeing to give you and get their signature to say they are gifting you some funds.

Family guarantee

Leading NSW mortgage broker Grace Bowen says the great news is that deposit assistance doesn't necessarily need to be in the form of cash but can also be via family offering their home as security. Family guarantees can help people save thousands of dollars in LMI and buy a house sooner even if they don't have the full deposit saved. Not all banks offer family guarantees, but a mortgage broker can advise which banks do.

Applying for pre-approval

Pre-approval is where a lender has agreed, in principle, to lend you money towards the purchase of your home up to a certain limit.

Pre-approvals are valid for around three months and help you know how much you're actually allowed to borrow so you won't waste time looking at properties you can't afford. Plus the real estate agent will take you a *lot* more seriously.

A mortgage broker can help you get pre-approval, as you need to pull a whole bunch of documents together, like your driver's licence, savings statements, tax returns and monthly expenses.

Mortgage broker Kathy Euers says most banks want to see one to three months of your transaction account that contains your living expenses for two reasons.

Reason 1: They want to see that you've got good account conduct (you don't let your account go into the negative).

Reason 2: To see whether there are any undisclosed liabilities. For example, you might have disclosed a car loan and a credit card but they want to see if there's anything else coming out of that account, as well as what you're spending each month.

Ninja money tip

Get your accounts into tip-top shape as some banks want to see three months' worth of statements. Credit cards can really impact your servicing capability so if you have a credit card with a big limit, cut the limit right down.

If you're self-employed

Kathy says the process is a little bit different because your income is received less all your expenses, leaving you with a net profit, plus any income you have paid yourself out this net profit. The banks and lender will look at your application and your business's financial position will also be taken into account; therefore, you also need to provide evidence such as company tax returns and other financial statements. As an example, if your total income is $100,000 but you have expenses of $80,000 (which includes your wage of $20,000), you are left with $40,000 of usable income. 'That's why I generally work longer with self-employed clients and their accountants closely for at least a year before they are looking to buy,' Kathy says.

What's the deal with credit scores?

Banks and lenders will look at your credit score to decide whether you're reliable and likely to pay back the loan. They will gather personal and financial information that's kept in a credit report. It might seem a bit stalkerish but they are just looking at your financial behaviours – if you have any debts or if you always pay your bills on time. They want to ensure they are going to get their money back.

You can apply for a free copy of your credit report from companies such as Experian, Illion and Equifax. A bad credit score is anything below 550. A good score is 700+ and anything around 800 is excellent. Obtaining a copy of your credit score won't affect your credit report – that's only if you make a credit enquiry (loans, credit cards etc.).

Three ways to improve your credit score:

- Have a steady source of income.
- Pay off your loans or debts on time.
- Build up your savings.

Three things that will negatively affect your score:

- Late and missed payments.
- Defaulted payments. Even once you pay the debt, the default will stay on your credit file for five years.
- Owing money on old bills, such as electricity or mobile bills (even if it's only 50 cents owing).

If your credit score comes back low, you can engage with a credit repair agency. Victoria Coster, CEO of Credit Fix Solutions, says, 'One in three Australians have bad credit, so if you come back low, don't worry, it's pretty common. You can engage with a credit fix agency to help you fix your report, they will do things like investigate negative data with credit providers and collect documents on the account on your behalf. Having a good report can mean saving thousands on interest repayment because the more traditional lenders usually require a score of 700 or above to access the best interest rates. People with bad credit, defaults and low credit scores cannot access the best interest rates, and have to go with lenders that are more expensive.'

Choosing a loan

It's during this stage that you'll pick the kind of loan you want. The two most common are fixed-rate and variable. You can also get a split loan, which is a combination of both. This is also where you will work out with your mortgage broker whether you're likely to pay back the principal and interest, or just the interest.

The principal of your home loan is the amount of money you borrow from your bank or lender. Principal and interest loans typically carry a lower interest rate and it means you're paying down your debt faster.

The interest is the cost charged to you by the bank or lender to borrow this money.

A **fixed-rate loan** means the interest rate stays the same for a certain time period. Kathy says, 'If you're fixing for four years, you need to be really sure that you're going to keep that property and/or loan for four years, as break costs can be high.' Fixed loans are good if interest rates are rising and for people who love to budget and know the exact amount they have to pay each month.

A **variable loan** has an interest rate that varies, meaning it changes over time.

It can go up or down as the lending market changes (e.g. when official cash rates change). It's then up to your bank whether they pass this change on to their customer or not.

With a variable rate, you can also have an offset account attached. It's a good option for those people who want to pay off their loan faster.

What is an offset account?

An offset account is just a transaction account that is linked to your home loan – the money in your offset account is offset against your home loan. If you've got $10,000 in the offset account then the amount of your home loan you're charged interest on is reduced by $10,000. Your home loan repayments don't change but you save on interest and it helps reduce your loan term. With money in an offset account, you might end up paying a 30-year loan off in 25 years instead.

Look for your dream home

Time for the fun part!

What's important to you? Consider things like:

- Location – Does it have good access to schools, cafes, public transport, parks and grocery shops?
- Infrastructure – Is there established infrastructure or plans to develop in the area?
- Suburb – Is it community-friendly?
- Type of property – House, unit, townhouse?
- Features – Number of bedrooms, bathrooms, backyard, parking?

Make an offer

When you find a property you like, you can then make an offer to the real estate agent. In a hot 'seller's market', where loads of people are snapping up properties fast, it will be a matter of putting your best offer in writing to the agent and accepting where possible the vendor's terms and conditions on the contract. For example, if the vendor wants a longer settlement of three or six months, can you accommodate that?

When the market cools off and becomes a 'buyer's market' there's a lot more opportunity for you to negotiate the asking price.

Private sale

This takes place when the property owner sets the base sale price and the real estate agent negotiates with buyers to achieve the highest possible sale price.

Real estate agent Jeff Uebergang says with a private sale the 'sellers set the price, the buyers set the terms'. During this time you can work with your conveyancer to ensure you have inserted your preferred clauses into the contract.

Auction

This is when buyers bid on a property at a fixed location and time. The highest bidder on the day purchases the property, as long as the bid matches or exceeds the reserve price (the price the sellers have set) and the bidder has 10% of the property price available as a deposit. Don't forget to get your pest control and building inspection done before auction day. Once that hammer comes down you own that property. After the auction, you have to organise for the bank to do the valuation. With auctions, sellers set the terms, the buyers set the price.

A cooling-off period is a period of time where you, the buyer, can withdraw from the sale without major legal or financial consequences. In New South Wales there's a cooling-off period of five days. Cooling-off periods do not apply when you're buying a property through an auction.

Sold!

Once you have signed the contract of sale, send a copy to your mortgage broker who will organise a valuation by your bank and start the process for formal approval.

Once you purchase a property and sign a contract, there's a very grey area about who actually owns that property if it goes up in flames. So set up your insurance as soon as you've exchanged or signed the contract. Some insurers offer 90 days of free insurance from signing through to settlement.

Final inspection

When the settlement period is nearly finished you are allowed a final inspection of the property. This is your last chance to check that the state of the property has not changed during the settlement period and that the agreed inclusions or exclusions have been left or removed from the property.

Settlement

Settlement day involves your conveyancer meeting with your lender and the seller's representatives to sign and exchange the final documents of the sale.

Land transfer duty or stamp duty is usually paid on the settlement date as well. The title to the property won't be transferred to your name until you have paid this duty.

The seller is responsible for rates and other council fees up to and including the day of settlement, but after this, you'll need to pay these costs.

Once settlement is completed, you can collect the keys from the agent and take possession of the property. It's time to move into your new home at last!

Three quick tips to repay your loan faster

1. **Use an offset account** to reduce the interest you pay.
2. **Make extra repayments.** If you paid an extra $200 per month you could reduce a 30-year loan (with a 2.5% interest rate) by three years and ten months and save over $30,000.
3. **Pay fortnightly.** There are 12 months or 52 weeks in a year which means you would be making 26 fortnightly repayments and are effectively making 13 monthly repayments in a 12-month period.

That's a wrap!

You have the steps now so you can start getting ready to jump on that property ladder. Sherry Smith, Prestige Property real estate expert of 20 years, says, 'The best time to buy real estate is today, time will look after you.'

To action with your gal pals

- ☐ Choose a mantra and say it out loud every day: 'I can afford to buy a house.' 'I will be a property owner.' 'Buying a home is within my grasp!'
- ☐ Set up your 'Dream House fund' and put the first dollar in there!
- ☐ Start looking at houses in areas you are interested in.

CHAPTER 11

Let's Talk About the Money, Honey

In the early stages of romance, when things are getting hot and heavy, raising the subject of money can be a real buzzkill.

When is the right time to have the money conversation? Okay, maybe not on the first Bumble date, but you also don't want to be walking down the aisle when you find out your love is up to their eyeballs in debt. We don't want you to catch any STDs (sexually transmitted debts). In this chapter, we'll give you some conversation-starters and strategies so you can confidently turn to your partner and say, 'Honey, it's time to talk about the money.'

Be the CFO of your life

Ladies, your money is something you can't outsource to your partner. You need to be the CFO (chief financial officer) in your life. Research from UBS showed that 98% of widows and divorcees would advise other women to take a more active role with their money. Your partner is not 'better at money' and once you hand your financial power over it can be very difficult to get it back. I speak to many women and men working in finance who are always amazed at how quickly the female clients hand over their money to their partners.

Talking about money leads to a happier relationship

Research shows that if you want to have a happy relationship you and your honey need to get aligned on the money. According to TD Bank's annual Love & Money Survey, couples of all ages are happier when they talk about money, and those who talk about it least are the unhappiest. It makes sense, right? Relationships Australia says financial stress is one of the leading contributors of separation in Australia.

If you have a partner, money will play a big role in your life together and you want to make sure you're on the same page.

Let's look at the different stages of a relationship and where and when you might want to be having certain 'talks'.

Stages of a relationship

Step 1 First date

Woohoo, it's the first date! The person opposite you is a giant cutie patootie, you've covered all the first date basics like where you grew up, siblings, what holidays you have planned, hard or soft taco preferences ... and then the bill comes out. Who pays the bill?

Emily Brooks, in her book *The First Move*, makes an excellent point that if you don't make an attempt to pay as they are reaching for their wallet, what your silence is saying is, 'I can be bought.' You're laying down unequal ground on which to build a relationship and the other person will take note.

Like the bill, this conversation can be split a few ways. If they asked you on the date, does that mean they pay? If you asked them, does that mean you have to pay? What if they are super boring or just talked about themselves, should they pay? If they ask you to the most expensive bar in town does that mean it's on them? So many questions ... it was just one meal!

My personal opinion is to split the first dinner or, if they insist on paying, be very clear that you will get the next one or the drinks. When I go on dates and I'm not interested in the other person, I will insist on paying half the bill or at least buying them a drink so I don't feel like I owe them anything. If I like them and they insist on paying, I let them know I'll get the next one.

Questions to ask:

- How do you want to split the bill?
- Do you want another date? (Smooth, right? 😂)

Step 2 We are now Facebook official

I know going Facebook official is not a thing anymore but this next stage is when you like each other and have decided you're not going to date other people.

While things are still new it's a great time to learn more about their money story and goals.

You can also pay attention to how they spend their money – are they ordering Uber Eats every evening? Do they like hitting up the fanciest cocktail bars? Do they drive a fancy car? Do they use a credit card?

I'm not saying being a big spender is a bad thing, especially if they can afford it. But their spending habits can be a telltale sign as to whether your values are aligned and if money is likely to become an issue as your relationship progresses.

Questions to ask:

- Do you have any holidays planned?
- Are you saving for anything?
- Do you prefer to cook or order takeaway?
- What's your favourite budgeting app? (Okay, maybe I'm a finance nerd.)

Step 3 Your first holiday together

Things are going well (yay!), and you decide you want to go on a romantic weekend away. This is a good chance to have another money conversation and also to look out for any red flags.

A good friend of mine, Jules, was dating this guy who wanted to take her away for an impromptu romantic weekend. It was out of her price range so she suggested they go somewhere a little more affordable, but he insisted. It was very nice and very fancy but when it came to the end, he conveniently realised he had forgotten his card (a common theme) and promised he would pay her back. A few weeks later when she asked if he could transfer her for his share, he got really defensive, then any time she brought it up he would start a fight. She later found out he had massive credit card debt and was a complete overspender, and their very different money priorities contributed to the relationship breaking up.

Questions to ask:

- How do you want to split expenses? If you pay for the hotel how about I pay for the flights and tours?
- Shall we track on Splitwise (app) 'cause I don't want you overpaying?
- Should we just put $X into a kitty and use that to pay for everything?

Step 4 Sharing a bed and a bank account

There will definitely have to be money conversations with your partner at the 'moving in' stage. It's inevitable, otherwise how will you know how to split bills, who's paying for the wi-fi, and what about the Jif and toilet paper? The good thing is that, generally, it's cheaper living as two because you get to split all those expenses.

This is a good opportunity to talk money because you can say you're excited to move in together but you would like to put some time aside one night to chat through the financial stuff.

I want to acknowledge that sometimes this can be an awks conversation at the start. 'Oh, you budget in your head? That's, err ... cool.' So when approaching this conversation, or if you start having 'money date nights', make sure you pick a space out of the home, avoid large amounts of alcohol and be open – try not to get defensive. A good place to start is chatting to each other about where you are at and sharing what you both earn, own, owe and spend.

A friend of mine does Wealthy Wednesday night with her partner where they talk about their money mangement, spending plan, savings and investment goals! I might add they are one of the happiest couples I know.

At Ladies Finance Club, we get asked *all* the time how to split finances with your partner. There are a lot of different approaches to this, especially if one of you earns more than the other. Here are some ways you can approach splitting expenses with your partner.

Option 1 – When you earn similar salaries

Keep your individual bank accounts (fun money, adulting fund, future me fund, expenses) but also open a joint account together. You'll use the joint account to pay for your shared household bills 50/50.

You might also want to have another joint account for holidays or special occasions.

Option 2 – When salaries are different

Add your individual incomes together to get your total household income. Then calculate the percentage of that total each partner makes.

Let's look at an example of Molly and Brad (*cough*, Pitt). Okay, so Brad works in movies and earns more than Molly who runs her own event company.

If Molly earns $65,000 a year while Brad is on $100,000 – that's a total income of $165,000.

Molly's total household income is $65,000 ÷ $165,000 = 39%

Brad's total household income is $100,000 ÷ 165,000 = 61%

Now add up all the expenses you've agreed to split. Then use the percentages to see how much you're each responsible for.

If monthly expenses (rent, bills, cleaner etc.) came to $3000:

Molly's portion is $3000 x 39% = $1170

Brad's portion is $3000 x 61% = $1830

Every month, both partners transfer their share into the joint account.

Some partners will be happy with this, others might find it unfair. This is where it's really important to have an open conversation and ensure everyone is happy with the arrangement. It's important you always have your own 'fun money' and never need to feel guilty or ask for permission to spend it!

What about big joint goals like saving for a house? Financial advisor and money coach Gemma Mitchell says you can be working together on a shared financial goal, like a home deposit, without a joint account or combining all aspects of your finances. Protecting yourself and your savings, in case things don't work out, is smart. And just like other areas of relationships, communication and clear boundaries around your finances are key.

Until you are married or considered in a de facto relationship (rule of thumb is around two years) it's important to keep major purchases separate and documented, because you don't have the same legal protections as married couples in case of a split. Keep track of who paid what towards every major purchase (like furniture and appliances) in a simple Excel spreadsheet, and keep your receipts.

Ninja money tip

Your emergency fund should always be in your own name, and only you should have access to it.

Questions to ask:

- Do we want to pay for a cleaner?
- Who is in charge of paying which bills?
- If you won a million dollars in the lottery, what would your first purchase be?
- What word would you use to describe your relationship with money?
- Is there a limit that we can spend in the joint account without needing each other's approval?

Step 5 Commitment

Getting married is a legal contract, which means what is mine is now yours. Having difficult conversations now, while things are good, will put you in good stead if things get rocky further down the road.

If your partner has debt

Debt is common and often at least one person is entering the marriage with debt. First, get clear on their level of debt and then come up with a plan to demolish it. Avoid making them feel guilty or bad about it. 'WHAT, how did you even get into that much debt?! Where did you spend it all?' isn't going to help the situation. Be open, listen and work through a plan using the snowball or avalanche method.

This is an exciting time to get aligned on your money goals as a couple. Research conducted by Ramsey Solutions found that a whopping 87% of respondents who say their marriage is 'great' also say they and their spouse work together to set long-term goals for their money.

To make it less intense, you can each fill out our couples' money questionnaire on the Ladies Finance Club resources page individually and then come back together to discuss the answers.

Questions to ask:

- What do you own (assets, property, investments)?
- Do you have any debts (student loans, credit cards, Buy Now Pay Laters)?
- How much do you have in super?
- Do you have a will?
- Would you lend money to a friend or family member in need?
- Do we have equal say on how we use our money, no matter who earns more?
- What are our retirement goals (what age and how much do you want to retire on)?
- What does being financially 'comfortable' look like to you?

Ninja money tip

Get paid into your account first.

Family Lawyer Tessa Kelman advises to always get paid into your own bank account first and then pay a portion into the joint account. In the unfortunate case of a separation, it makes it much easier for you to have a clear sense of who has paid what.

Should you get a prenup?

We are settling down later in life. This means you might be bringing more than your charms and charisma to the table – you may have property, investments, a full super fund or may even be expecting a large inheritance. It can be smart to talk about a prenup or, as we call them in Australia, a binding financial agreement (BFA) to protect your assets. This doesn't mean either party thinks the relationship is going to fail or that they are doomed from the start, it just means they are being smart and practical. Yes, it's probably going to be an awkward conversation because we all want to believe that we will marry our one true love forever. But one in three marriages will end in divorce. Some ways of starting the conversation could be: 'My family and I have always discussed that if I were to get a property or inheritance I would need to sign a BFA,' or, 'I watched a friend go through a messy divorce and lawyers said it would have been so much easier had there been a BFA in place.' Relationships have broken up over this one, so approach it carefully.

Financial abuse

In Australia up to 16% of women will experience financial abuse in their lifetime. It doesn't matter your age, where you live, your sexual orientation, social class or education – financial abuse doesn't discriminate.

Financial abuse is a type of family violence and involves withholding money, controlling household spending or refusing to include you in financial decisions. The vast majority of cases are men abusing women.

- Does your partner monitor what you spend?
- Do you feel scared to ask for money?
- Does your partner make you feel stupid or that you can't be trusted with money?
- Does your partner stop you from earning your own money or going to work?

- Are your household loans, mortgages, credit cards and accounts only in one person's name?
- Are they pressuring you to take on a loan or a debt on their behalf?

If you or someone you know is experiencing financial abuse, there are free services you can access in Australia:

- 1800RESPECT on 1800 737 732.
- Good Shepherd Australia Financial Independence Hub, 1300 050 150, 9am to 5pm, Monday to Friday.
- National Debt Helpline, 1800 007 007, 9.30am to 4.30pm, Monday to Friday.

That's a wrap!

Even though it might be awkward, it's important that you and your honey talk about the money. The conversation can start and continue from the first date. If you're really struggling to broach the topic, there are financial coaches who work with couples to get aligned on goals and spending rules. Remember the couples that talk about money (and are aligned on the same financial goals) stay together!

To action with your gal pals

If you are in a relationship:

- ☐ Lock in a time with your honey when you can talk about money and put it into your calendars (go to a nice cafe, to the park or another neutral space).
- ☐ Get clear on your #CoupleGoals: use the template from Chapter 3 to plan your short, medium and long-term goals together.
- ☐ Download our 21 questions to ask your partner about money PDF from ladiesfinanceclub.com/money.

If you are single:

- ☐ Be aware of your money story and any limiting beliefs you might be bringing into any of your relationships, whether friendships or future partnerships.

CHAPTER 12

The Parent Trap

Want your kid to be a zillionaire? Or maybe just have some great financial foundations you wish you were taught. Well, no pressure but you can play a key role in shaping your children's feelings, thoughts and values about money and give them a head start (like you didnt have enough on your plate!).

As we move to a cashless society and money is 'invisible' it makes teaching kids about money a little bit more challenging. Post-Covid, retail and restaurants look at you like you're about to infect them if you hand over physical money.

In a world where you can buy pretty much anything instantly on your mobile, it's super important we are teaching kids proper money management. One Canberra family had a massive shock after they found their child had racked up $8000 purchasing fake food for his virtual pets via the dad's iPad where his card details were pre-saved.

How your children learn about money isn't something you want to leave up to chance or trial and error. If your children have seen you put everything on a credit card and stress about money this will affect their money mindset (remember Chapter 1).

Let's look at some ways to teach them good money skills.

1 Get your kids to join the conversation early

Research from the University of Cambridge found that most kids have formed their adult money behaviours by age seven. A study by the University of Wisconsin also found that kids can grasp basic economic concepts such as value and exchange by the age of three.

Money experts all agree you should *talk* to your kids about money.

Take the time to go through the bills or grocery lists as a family. This is also a great time to talk about needs versus wants. We want strawberry milk but we need milk. We need to pay the power bill but the Disney channel is nice to have.

The language you use matters so avoid using negative phrases like 'It's too expensive' or 'We can't afford it!' Children may connect money with negative feelings. Next time your kid is harassing you for a crappy toy, try to make it not about the money but the choice. If they have a goal like saving for a bike then explain buying the toy means they will have to wait longer for the bike. The point is it's not because you can't afford it but because you're choosing not to buy it. (I understand that when a child is having a meltdown in the supermarket it might be tricky to explain about gratitude and delayed gratification.)

2 Show your kids how money works

Talk to your children about how money works and what you do for money. Explain how and why you go to work and where your income comes from.

It can be helpful for your kids to be involved in purchases, especially big-ticket items like a new car. Beth Kobliner, *New York Times* bestselling author of *Make Your Kid a Money Genius (Even If You're Not)*, says this will allow them to observe your decision-making process and see your family's priorities and values in action. You might talk through what sort of features your family needs in a car, what things you want and what your budget is.

3 Define chore time

I am not here to tell you how to parent (although my hypothetical kids are a dream), but giving your kids household jobs should be part of everyday life. There were jobs I had to do as a kid, just because I was part of the family. They certainly weren't glamorous jobs: feeding the dogs, watering the plants, unloading the dishwasher or, my least favourite, emptying the compost. Pocket money should be kept separate from chores as the psychology changes when you link chores to pocket money.

Beth Kobliner says, 'If you tie chores to pocket money, that money becomes an external motivator for them – and worst of all, paying for chores can backfire. At some point, your kid may not see the value of making their bed or cleaning the dishes for $5. So keep the allowance and chores separate.'

Well said, Beth, we agree!

For many kids, pocket money will be the first time they have had to 'manage any money' so we want to give them some good foundations.

Every time I was given money as a child it was so common to hear, 'What are you going to buy?', 'What are you going to spend it on?' but we need to wire our kids' brains for better habits.

Ninja money tip

Do you find you never have cash on you? Some families use 'play money' and then the kids can substitute it for real money when they want to buy something.

We love the three piggy banks rule where you have three piggy banks (or virtual accounts). When the child is given any money they divide it up into their three piggy banks. If Grandma gives little Eloise $20 (thanks Granny), Eloise can then decide how she wants to split it into the three piggy banks – the only rule is she must contribute to all three piggy banks:

Saving – This is money to save up for something that they really want. It's so simple but teaches patience, delayed gratification and goal setting. Help your child come up with a goal that they want to save for – like a bike or entry into Movie World. For extra points, make a mini vision board with an image of their goal or download the Ladies Finance Club kids' money goal tracker and stick it on the fridge.

Sharing – This teaches your child gratitude and helping those in need. Work out what matters to your child and where to share!

Researchers at Stony Brook University and Harvard found that genuine giving makes you happier, helps with depression and is contagious in the community – now that's a virus I want to catch! #PhilanthropyPerks

Spending – Sometimes it's just fun to spend money. This is money for the 'now' such as getting an ice-cream or those fidgety spinner things. Kids can learn in a safe space about the value of money and get an early lesson in the difference between cheap products and quality goods. Hopefully this will also help with the nagging in the supermarket: 'Do you want to use your spending money on this?'

 Welcome to the adult world

Take your child to set up a bank account – you can turn this into a bit of an adventure followed by a milkshake! Explain how a bank works (you can keep it high level – a place that holds your money like at Gringotts). Okay, I get that for an actual adult going to a bank isn't that exciting, but for a kid, this could be one of their first steps into adulthood. Even if you only bank online, you can still do it together at the computer and make it special. Discuss why it's a good thing and agree on a savings goal!

To open a bank account in Australia kids under the age of 13 years will need a parent or guardian to help them set up their account online or at a branch. Kids aged 14 years or older can open a bank account themselves (some banks differ).

5 The gender pay gap starts at home

If you do decide to give pocket money, don't let gender get in the way. It might sound crazy but the gender pay gap for many females starts at home, with girls doing more of the unpaid labour like helping out with the cleaning and caring roles. Girls' clothes, shoes and cosmetics are usually more expensive (the pink tax) so parents sometimes balance this out with giving the boys more money. A study also found that parents are less likely to allow girls control of their own finances, while boys are given regular payments, teaching them to manage their money. This is also seen and reflected in the media with articles about women's savings focusing on being frugal (do your own nails) while men's articles discuss growing wealth through property and investments. I heard a story once about how a girl would get a doll as a present from her grandma while her brother would get $50 cash. This is slowly changing, but not fast enough, so make sure you're checking your own biases.

Practical activities you can do with your kids

Ages 3 to 10

Play shop: When I was a kid, I would set up a little store in my bedroom and get my siblings to buy books from me with play money. By exchanging play money for goods, your child begins to understand the basics of commerce.

Big notes can break down: Show them how big notes can be broken into the smaller amounts.

Checkout kid: When you get to the checkout line, let your kid pay. Hand them the cash or your card and explain to them that money you have already earned is being taken from your account to pay for the groceries.

The magic money machine: When you withdraw money from an ATM, explain that this is money you had to earn. Some kids think ATMs are free money machines. #WeWish

Ages 10 to 13

What business could it be: When passing empty shops get the kids to brainstorm business ideas for the space. This will help grow their entrepreneurial mind to look for opportunities.

How much is that doggy in the window: Get your child to research how much owning a pet costs (grooming, registration, vet bills, food etc.).

Find me the best deal: Ask your kids to help you look for the best deals on things like toilet paper and soap powder in the supermarket!

Let's play: Board games are a fun way to teach kids about money. Good money games include Pay Day, Squatter (the most Aussie game you can play!), Exchange, Monopoly (warning: does trigger family fights) and Pocket Money. There are a heap of online games as well!

Mini Buffetts: Tell your kids to choose a company they know (Disney, Google, McDonald's, Nike, Netflix etc.). Explain what a share is (a part of a company you can buy) and make a note of the price. You can turn it into a competition as the share prices go higher or lower over a period of time.

Party time: Get them to organise their own birthday party with a mini-budget (cake, balloons, games etc). Although as a child if I had to choose between a karaoke machine and face painting it would have been a tough call.

No frills: When at the supermarket, explain the difference between brand and non-brand items and how they are the same products often made up of the same ingredients but one is more expensive than the other.

Ages 13 to 16

Get a job! Encourage your child to get a part-time job as it will help teach them responsibility, work ethic and teamwork, and it will be their first slice of financial independence pie. This is also a great way to start a conversation about super, the benefits of compounding and how they are already investing their money (they just can't touch it for a long time!).

Talk about tax: Tax gets a bad rap and most of us start a pretty nego relationship with tax when we realise that this 'tax' person has taken a chunk of our money. We never want to pay too much tax but it's good to talk about how tax pays for roads, parks and healthcare.

I spy fuel with my little eye: As you drive around in the car, start getting your kids to look at petrol prices and note the difference from station to station, or if you need to fill up, get the kids to jump on a website or app to find the cheapest fuel in the area! Ah, isn't it nice when technology and kids are working together for the greater good of your wallet?

The dangers of borrowing money: Show them the dangers of credit cards using an example of buying a $1000 laptop on credit and only paying off the minimum balance. How much would you spend in interest and how long it would take? (Assuming an 18% credit card rate, it would be seven years and nine months!) You can find links to credit card calculators on our website.

Broom broom: Bestselling author Anthony O'Neal suggests encouraging children to save for a car by matching 50% of what they save. Help them work out how much they will need to save, how much they will need to earn and how long it will take them.

Mini boss: Get the entrepreneurial juices flowing and encourage your kids to start their own business. If you can teach them early business concepts then your children will be in front of the pack!

Small business ideas for kids:

- Sell homemade food products
- Wash cars
- Babysit
- Pet-sit
- Mow the lawn
- IT support – let's face it, most kids know more about technology than their parents ever will. Encourage them to put this knowledge to work for them.
- Jewellery making

Ninja money tip

Sydney-based financial advisor Rachel O'Connor says that when teaching your kids about investing, 'The first thing to think about is what you are trying to achieve by investing. If the purpose is to involve your child and teach them about investing you might use one strategy and one type of product.' If your purpose is to build up a pot of funds to cover some of the expenses relating to raising your child, such as their school fees, you may use a totally different strategy and product. Spriggy is a mobile app with a linked prepaid card that helps kids learn the concept of digital money. You can also invest for your kids via Spriggy's invest feature. Stockspot, Superhero, Sharesies, Pearler and SelfWealth also have options where you can open up an account for your child – just watch out for any tax implications and fees.

That's a wrap!

I love this saying by Andy Andrews: 'Remember, the goal is not to raise great kids; it's to raise kids who become great adults.' There are so many ways to get your child involved in financial decisions so make sure you're talking about money to your kid and not shying away from the conversation. Remember, a child's money mindset is made up by the time they are seven years old so how you behave and what you say can stick with them for a very long time!

To action with your gal pals

- ☐ Set up the three piggy bank rule.
- ☐ Decide if you're going to start investing for your kids now.
- ☐ If you don't have kids of your own, then remember you can always show your godkids, nieces and nephews how to start investing! #CoolAunt

CHAPTER 13

Mind the Gap

The first time I negotiated my salary I was 25, my heart was pounding, I had sweaty hands, I felt physically sick and I had all the nerves … I was shaking so badly that my boss thought I was about to break some terrible news.

I stumbled through a speech about why I deserved a pay rise. I was worried my boss would think I was being greedy or that maybe I wasn't deserving of it (although I had been working super hard and been doing way more than my original job description). I walked away with a 13% salary increase (self-five!).

There is nothing more disheartening than working in a job where you feel like you're not being paid your worth, or where you know your colleagues are being paid more than you for the same role. Women are still earning, on average, $261.50 less than men per week. Ladies, it's 2022. You have to negotiate your salary.

We talked earlier about how inflation is forecast to sit around 2% to 3%. If your company says, 'We are giving everyone a 3% pay rise,' that's not a pay rise, that's just ensuring you don't earn less than you did the year before.

Here are six steps to help you become a badass salary negotiator!

Step 1 Prepare

Going for a pay rise isn't something you do on a whim, it's something you have to prep for at least three to six months in advance. Do your research to find out what the same role is going for in similar companies. You can do this by using websites like Glassdoor, Seek, Payscale or by talking to recruiters. I did this a lot when I was living in London and applying for roles. I would call up recruiters and ask them what the salary range was, then always take the highest figure as market value. If you're asking friends who work in similar industries, Meggie Palmer, founder of PepTalkHer, says to ask for a range – 'Between X and X' – as friends might feel more comfortable to share.

Action: Call up a recruiter and ask them for a salary range on a similar job and industry you're in. Is it close to what you're currently on?

Step 2 Why you deserve a pay rise

Once you have established yourself as a hardworking, badass, smart employee (rule of thumb: at least 6 to 12 months after beginning a new role), start pulling together evidence of why you deserve a pay rise. Have you brought $100,000 worth of new work to the business? Did you get really good feedback from a client, nail a pitch or throw an amazeballs Xmas party? If you're prepping for a brand-new role at a different company you can do the same: use statistics, real examples and tangible results.

Action: Set a calendar reminder at 4pm on Friday and list out three of your biggest achievements for that week in an Excel doc, G-sheet or using the PepTalkHer app. You can use this as evidence later when you negotiate your salary. Keep it up to date. As Meggie Palmer says, 'I can't recall what I had for dinner most nights so it's likely your boss won't remember everything you've done.' They have multiple staff members to manage so keep yourself front of mind by sending them weekly or monthly wrap-ups of your achievements.

Action: Email your boss a summary of what you have achieved that week or month and then tell them where your focus will be for the following week/month.

Step 3 Choose the right time

Don't wait for your boss to notice all the work and long hours you've been doing and nominate you for a pay rise, it's more likely you're going to have to bring this topic up.

Good opportunities to do this include when you have a performance review or have finished a big project. If your company is making redundancies or if they are experiencing major operational issues, it's probably not a good time.

Book in a meeting with your manager so they can prepare – you don't want to spring this on them at the photocopier or after-work drinks. Meggie Palmer says, 'Put some time in your boss's calendar – send them an email and let them know you're looking forward to discussing your achievements and contribution to the team.'

Psychology Today says Thursdays are the best days to ask for a pay rise.

Action: Ask HR when salaries are reviewed and schedule a time with your boss to discuss yours or send yourself a diary reminder to set up a meeting in the future.

Step 4 Set your price

You have done your research and you know your market value, so get clear on how much more you want. Once you have your desired price, make sure you add a bit of a cushion on top, and avoid giving a range. If you want to buy a car and they said you could have it for $10,000 to $15,000, you'd say, 'I'll take it for $10,000 thanks.' Put your number out there first – this is known as anchoring and the psychology behind it is the first number offered is the number that will then be up for discussion. So if you're wanting $60,000 and they say, 'We were thinking $50,000,' the number is anchored to $50,000 and you might reduce your amount and say, 'I was thinking $55,000.' If you go in first with the number you want (plus a bit extra: $65,000) the number is anchored to that. If they were thinking $55,000, they may up it to $60,000.

When working out your 'want price' make sure you have worked out if it includes super or not! I have spoken to many a lady who took a job but hadn't realised super was included in the amount.

Action: With a friend, role-play asking for a salary increase and get them to accept, reject and question you on the pay rise.

Step 5 The meeting

You've done your prep, you know what price you're after and you've got your evidence as to why you deserve that figure. Some people like to write a mini agenda for the meeting so they don't miss anything important and I have been known to create a little presentation of what I have achieved (but that is a little extra)! When walking into your meeting, walk proud and tall (do some power poses in the toilet beforehand to get your confidence pumping). You've got what it takes to get that money!

It's likely one of three things will happen:

1. They will accept your offer – yippee, happy days!
   Action: Follow up with an email stating what you discussed and agreed upon, and from when the new compensation will start.
2. They will say they have to check the budget or with their manager.
   Action: Follow up with an email of what was discussed.
3. They will decline.
   Action: Are there any other benefits you can negotiate such as a job title, flexible working hours, additional annual leave? A 'no' might also mean a no for now, so this shouldn't put you off asking again in six months' time. You can also ask what you need to do to get a pay rise and then start putting a plan together.

If you're going for a role and they offer you an amount you're not happy with, don't feel pressured into saying yes straight away, instead thank them and say you will consider it. If they offer you an amount you really don't agree with, Tori Dunlap, founder of Her First 100K, recommends you use this script that helped her negotiate $10,000 more on a previous role:

'Thank you so much for this offer, I would love to join the team. Based on my skills, experience and the market salary rate, it would make sense for me to be in a higher range of $__________ to __________. If you could increase the offer by $10,000, I'd be eager to accept.'

NEGOTIATION INSPIRATION

Thank you so much. I'm excited to work with you and the team. I'm going to take some time to review the offer and I'll get back to you by COB today.

Thanks [name], my understanding is that the best you can offer for this role is $_______. I can accept that with a compensation package that includes an extra week of holiday and the potential to revisit my salary six months after being hired. If you're happy with those terms, I would love to come on board.

I really appreciate the offer and I'm excited about the possibility of being part of your team. As you are aware, I have been discussing job opportunities at other companies. If you're able to move the pay to $_______ I'd be eager to accept.

Thank you so much for the offer. I'm excited to get started and be part of the team. However, I was hoping we could discuss my compensation. Combined with my qualifications and experience, and what I've been seeing in market for similar roles right now, I would be comfortable accepting a salary of $_______ for this position.

I do believe there's a bit of a gap here, and I need to consider the fair market value for this role and the specific skills I'll be bringing to the table. I've been seeing what the market's like for similar roles right now, and it's more in the $A–Z range. Can we work something out closer to that?

That's a wrap!

If your house was worth $500,000 and someone offered you $300,000 you wouldn't accept it. When it comes to everyday negotiations – like who's making dinner or which Netflix show to watch – we are all pretty natural negotiators, but when it comes to negotiating a salary it's a different story! Research shows when women have to negotiate on behalf of someone else they are really good at it, so start negotiating for your future self, your kids, your partner and your fur baby! Men are also four times more likely than women to ask for a raise.

If you're not negotiating your salary then you're telling the world you don't think you're worth fighting for and that is BS. So get prepped and go get that money! Kayne West running for president was a great reminder that men look at a job description and think, 'Yeah, I could do that.' Ladies, you don't have to have all the skills. Apply for that job!

To action with your gal pals

- ☐ Find out when you each last negotiated your salary and if you're due for a review.
- ☐ Set up a Word or Excel doc, or download PepTalkHer, and schedule a reminder each Friday afternoon to write down your top wins for the week.

CHAPTER 14

Untying the Knot!

If you're unhappy and you know it (but don't want to have to start from scratch and take a massive financial hit), clap your hands!

We know that both divorce and separation will have a massive financial impact on your life and we want you to be in the best position to come out on top.

Nobody gets married thinking it will end. Relationship breakdowns are hard, emotionally and financially. Particularly if you are in a relationship where you have been given very little financial information or control.

There are processes in place that facilitate the exchange of financial information between spouses. Sydney-based family lawyer Samantha Lewis says, 'Don't be fooled if your partner suggests you don't need disclosure and that you can work it out just the two of you – it's like splitting a bill in a cafe without having the list of items and prices in front of you.'

When you circle back to being single, there's a list of must-dos: seeing a lawyer, dividing your assets and visiting your hairdresser for a radical new look. This chapter will cover the areas that need attention during a split, including spouse maintenance, property settlement and child support. It also shares advice from leading family lawyers Tessa Kelman and Shaya Lewis-Dermody about how to prepare yourself for a financially healthy split.

Before you separate

If your relationship is on the verge of ending, take some time to figure out your financial status first. The very first step is to get the details for all your bank accounts, particularly the ones in both your names. You may also need to review whether or not your accounts need joint permission for transactions.

'I have seen relationships end and one person decide to withdraw all the cash from an account,' Tessa says. 'It creates a big imbalance in power. I tell people to make sure you both have to sign to withdraw money so your partner can't take funds that you're entitled to.'

Shaya adds that it also helps to be aware of what's going on with your partner's business. 'Try to access tax statements and accounting information, and keep copies of documents.'

A recent Ladies Finance Club survey showed that 33% of women don't know how much their partner earns.

If you're in a relationship where you don't feel safe, you might not feel comfortable approaching your partner for this kind of information. At the very least, try to have the account details and statements, and talk to your banker about how your accounts are set up.

The same applies to investment properties and other significant assets. Take copies of statements, grab photos of valuable items and keep a record of everything you can find. It is your information but you risk losing access to it if you leave your home. Your partner may react to the separation by moving money if they feel angry or threatened. It is easier to prove your financial claims when you have photos of account balances and have downloaded transaction histories.

According to Tessa, 'There is a duty of disclosure in family law. As soon as there's a separation, you each need to disclose your financial circumstances, joint or solo, to the other person. That includes bank accounts, super statements, investment property records, everything to do with what's in your name, debt, super or assets.

'However, sometimes people just won't comply with this, even after a court order. So I say to people, particularly women, where their partner has been in control of everything, just a little bit of self-help before one of you leaves home is often better than trying to trawl through the courts to get them to disclose.'

COLLATE FINANCIAL DOCUMENTATION

The types of documents you may need include:

- [ ] Marriage certificate
- [ ] Birth certificates for your children
- [ ] Bank account statements
- [ ] Loan account and mortgage statements
- [ ] Insurance policies (health, home and contents, car, income protection and life)
- [ ] Tax records (tax returns and notices of assessment)
- [ ] Superannuation statements
- [ ] Car registration details
- [ ] Utility bills (gas, electricity and telephone)
- [ ] Property documents (leases, deeds and mortgage documents)
- [ ] Investment statements (managed funds or shares)
- [ ] Government benefit documents

Shaya's advice is to reach out to a family lawyer as early as you can. 'You don't have to tell your partner you're doing it,' she says. 'It will help you to avoid being overwhelmed.'

If the idea of paying for a lawyer is worrying you, Shaya says there are 'unbundled' options. Instead of paying for start-to-finish service, you can pay a fixed fee for shorter consultations. 'An unbundled service might be one-off legal advice before you go to mediation, or if you think you've reached an agreement, you take it to the lawyer to draft up properly.'

Finally, Shaya says it is a good idea to think about what's important to you. 'Do you want to stay in your home? Do you want to buy somewhere else? How much co-parenting do you want to do? Nobody really "wins" in divorce but if you know what you want most, your lawyer can help you to work towards it.' Hot tip: give your mortgage broker a quick call and find out if you can afford house repayments by yourself.

The divorce 'umbrella'

Technically, a divorce is administrative: the removal of a marriage certificate. It's a paperwork process that you can complete after you have formally separated for 12 months.

Divorce itself is straightforward and relatively affordable. Once the steps are complete, you're free to marry again and you can refer to yourself as single. The process to determine child care arrangements, financial support and the division of assets is where things become complicated.

When you separate, you will need to agree on property settlement, spouse maintenance and arrangements for child care, if you have children. The aim is to resolve everything more or less in unison.

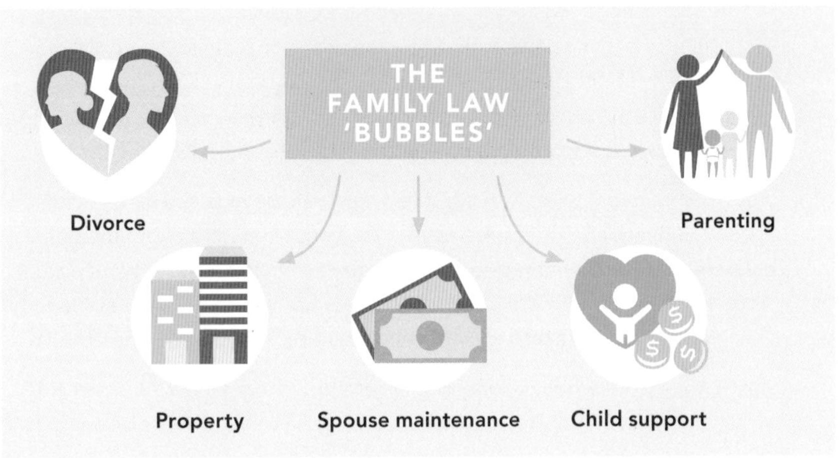

Spouse maintenance

Spouse maintenance comes into play when one party requires financial support from the other after the separation. For example, a mum with young children who has been out of the workforce. It's not possible for her to move out with no income, especially if the assets are yet to be divided.

Your money may be tied up in the family home when you separate and until it is sold you will have to either manage the cost of living in it yourself or access the funds you need to live somewhere else. The separation process will ask how much money you need and whether your ex has the capacity to pay you (or vice versa).

It's best to reach an agreement about spouse maintenance without going to court. 'A lawyer might make a recommendation to a client about what's appropriate, which will then go to the former partner. If there is an agreement, that's great. If not, the next step is to go to court,' says Tessa.

Child care and child support

In Australia, family lawyers talk about 'care arrangements' rather than custody of children. You will need to agree on who will look after the children and when. Many couples split this 50/50, while others have a weekend or school holiday arrangement.

The intersection with property settlement comes when the children live either full time or the majority of the time with one person. If this is the case, the person doing the majority of caring will need financial compensation.

Child support can be complicated, but it exists, in theory, to ensure the needs of children are met after a separation.

One option is to do an online child support assessment, which tells you what you each need to pay after analysing your earnings and care arrangements. You can also reach a private agreement.

Child support is divided into 'periodic' – which covers day-to-day needs like food, groceries, transport – and 'non-periodic', which covers things like school fees, medical, orthodontics. Generally, the goverment's online child support assessment formula only provides for periodic expenses. This is why there need to be agreements around things like private schools and how they will be paid for.

Once child support is decided on, the person who owes the money can either pay privately or the money will be deducted automatically from their pay.

One more thing: while you may not be concerned about your ex leaving the country with your children, it can be helpful to hand important documents like birth certificates and passports to a reliable third party (like a lawyer) for safekeeping during the separation procedure. This way nobody can 'weaponise' the kids.

Property settlement

Factors around spouse maintenance, child care and child support all contribute to the final property settlement. The way assets are distributed will depend on the ability of each partner to support themselves financially after the relationship has ended and the amount of money they need to care for existing children. The amount each person contributed during the relationship and the assets they commenced the relationship with will also come into play in a property settlement.

In family law, a balance sheet is used to clarify financial information. This is a standard court document that demonstrates the value of your assets and liabilities, including cash, property, investments and superannuation.

You can do this on your own, but make sure you think of everything. 'Superannuation is often missed because people don't think it's an asset,' Tessa says, 'but super still goes in the mix and should be divided up based on what's fair for either party.'

Even an amicable agreement can leave you missing out on money you are entitled to without realising it. When you get professional help, everything will be documented then weighed up based on a range of factors.

Tessa explains, 'Another situation I encounter is people who come to me a year after separating. They tell me that they made quick decisions without any help because they just wanted to move on. They later realise that what they agreed to wasn't fair. The good news is that if they haven't made things legally binding, we can potentially unpack it.'

UPDATE YOUR ACCOUNTS, WILL AND SUPERANNUATION

- ☐ If you do not already have one, you may wish to open a separate bank account in your name
- ☐ You should change your PIN and online banking passwords
- ☐ Try to reach agreement about the use of joint bank accounts and credit cards (including an agreement for two to sign)
- ☐ Update your insurance policies and superannuation binding death nomination forms so that your insurance and superannuation goes to your intended beneficiaries
- ☐ Update your estate plan including your will, power of attorney and enduring guardianship documents

What are you entitled to?

The tricky part of a divorce comes in dividing everything fairly.

If you end up in court, each individual's contributions are reviewed. The court will check how much cash was contributed during the relationship and how much each person contributed to property repayments.

Non-financial contributions, in the form of home-making and parenting, also count. Even if you weren't employed while with your partner, you are entitled to your share of money from the relationship.

Final decisions also take future needs into account. If you're a mother who has three children under five and can't work full-time but your ex is earning $300,000 per year, this gets considered.

One more thing to take into account is timing. You can't formally divorce someone then come back after three years and lay claim to their money. Your lawyer can talk to you about timing but it is generally a year from the time of divorce or two years after you ended a de facto relationship.

Making things official

Why do things by the book? Consider a scenario where you and your ex agree verbally to send your children to a private school. If they change their mind and there is nothing in writing, there won't be much you can do about it when they no longer agree to help pay the fees.

Shaya encountered a divorced woman who lived in a granny flat on her husband's property after they split. 'He had said, "I will always look after you" but after ten years, he decided to sell. Her application to the court for some of the money was unsuccessful because it had been so long since they ended their relationship.'

Simply signing the divorce declaration isn't enough. You need to resolve things more officially so you don't face the risk of losing money down the road.

Mediation

Ending a relationship is a buzzkill (to put it lightly). Many couples find they can't decide who is entitled to what in an amicable way. A mediator will help achieve positive outcomes for both of you.

Bring your lawyer with you if you don't feel comfortable attending mediation alone. You could also skip the meetings and have your lawyer mediate on your behalf.

The purpose of mediation is to resolve the details of your separation without requiring intervention in a court setting. Ideally, after some back and forth, you'll be able to reach win–win agreements and get on with living your new life.

There are low cost options for mediators, such as Relationships Australia and other family relationship centres, or you can find someone who specialises in this area.

'Remember to wear your business hat when negotiating,' says Shaya. 'Be courteous, polite and business-like. It can go a long way to trying to resolve your matter quickly and cost-effectively.'

Going to court

An amicable separation saves money, time and stress.

Mediation is the compulsory first step during a separation, but court is the backup. The judge will impose orders, often to revisit the mediation process in a different way (there are court-appointed mediators), or to do what your lawyer has suggested might be appropriate anyway.

Your family lawyer will be the person who represents you and does the 'day-to-day' court work. You might be wondering about the scenes you see in the movies with separating couples sitting behind desks in front of a judge; this is what happens after unsuccessful mediation, conciliation and other steps over several months or even a couple of years. It's not actually common to reach this point.

The movie and TV depiction of people refusing to sign divorce papers is also not accurate. In reality, you simply have to serve your partner with the documents.

Shaya reminds us that court is where the costs start to add up. 'Things get very slow. If you can avoid court, do so because you will end up with a judge making decisions for you and the entire situation becomes so much more stressful.'

Couples who reach court usually do so because there is a great deal of conflict, a history of family violence or one party refusing to 'play ball' when it comes to mediation. However, the court's jurisdiction is very powerful and the decisions may not work out in your favour. 'The judge can make an order that a house be sold if someone doesn't engage in court proceedings,' Shaya explains.

Don't forget!

Shaya recommends reviewing your will and life insurance policy after you separate from your partner. 'People get divorced and forget to remove their partner as their nominated beneficiary or the executor of their estate. It's a simple process to update these documents and have them witnessed and signed.'

That's a wrap!

Divorce can herald an exciting new chapter. Hopefully, you will find the right help and separate your finances and lives in a way that works out for everyone. It may feel difficult but there is always a light at the end of the tunnel. Self-care is a very important step, so make sure you look after your mental and physical health! There are even dedicated 'divorce coaches' to get you through the hard times.

To action with your gal pals

Whether you're going through a divorce or not, it's good to be prepared:

- ☐ Take photos of all your paperwork.
- ☐ If you're thinking of separating, arrange a meeting with a family lawyer (and yes, take your gal pal along to take notes).

The Final Wrap

Well, it's been a hot minute. It might be the end of the book but it's the beginning of your money journey (naw)! We don't have to be scared about talking about money and we don't have to feel guilty, anxious or confused. Make the time to look after your money now and your money will look after you later.

There are a few key takeaways I wanted to leave you with for this final wrap.

1 Remember that you're the only one responsible for your finances

I get that it's easy to hand over responsibility to someone, I know you're busy and time poor, but you now have all the skills you need to manage your own money.

We have to be across our finances and can't hand over our financial power to our partner. If you're still struggling with taking full control, seek external help. When we are sick, we see a doctor; when a pipe bursts, we use a plumber; if we want to get fit, we get a PT or join a gym. If you need help with your finances, you can see a money coach or debt counsellor – you don't have to struggle by yourself.

We as women are still fighting for equality and for equal pay. It wasn't until the 1970s that Australian women could even open a bank account or get a mortgage without a male guarantor. We can't give this control up – we fought too hard for it.

2 Your money has power

In Australia, women are leading the charge in ethical investing. Women are now earning more than we ever have, and we will see more and more wealth transfer to women because as women live longer, men will pass control of their assets over to their partners. Where you put that money can have a positive or negative effect on the environment or social issues. Use your money and help build a greener, cleaner, kinder world – you can opt out from investing in fossil-fuel, weapons, gambling and tobacco industries. Take the time to investigate where your retirement savings and investments are being used. If these don't align with your values then make the switch. You can also use your money to invest in or donate to causes that you're passionate about. When we have complete financial control, we can do so much good.

3 Your goals might not happen overnight

When we start saving and investing, we might not see results for a long time. That's the thing – investing isn't about getting rich overnight. Look at compounding interest for example: after ten years of investing $100 a month (with an average return of 8%) you would have $17,384 – but keep up the same rate of investment and in another ten years you would have $54,914 and in another ten years again, $135,940. It's about consistency and not trying to time the market. Warren Buffett was worth $100 million at 50 years old but grew his wealth to $86 billion by the time he reached 90. Time is your friend.

Want more?

If you're ready to start growing your wealth, I would love to invite you into the Ladies Finance Club. We run monthly masterclasses, have accountability groups, mini courses and events, and it's a great place to learn about investing now that you have the basics down pat! It's a safe space where you can ask your questions and join a community of other like-minded women who are all ready to get money savvy and take real control over their futures! Please feel free to create your own Ladies Finance Club with your girlfriends – no one loses when women have money. Use these catch-ups to talk about investments, tax, wills, how you manage money and talk about all #TheMoneyThings. Remember that money is something we use every day and spend a lot of time earning, so we have to make talking about money way less taboo.

Remember too that this is your one life and you can totally do this. There are so many incredible women in the world who are willing to help you if you ask.

Take care and go get 'em, tiger!

Big Love,

Molly xxx

Useful Resources

For more links to our favourite resources, tools, templates and calculators mentioned in the book, head over to ladiesfinanceclub.com/money.

Debt

- **National Debt Helpline** – 1800 007 007 for free and confidential advice from professional financial counsellors.
- Aboriginal and Torres Strait Islander peoples can call the free **Mob Strong Debt Helpline** on 1800 808 488.
- **Moneycare** offer free financial counselling – contact them on 1800 722 363.
- Money coaching is great for women looking to change their habits – email hello@ladiesfinanceclub.com to get in touch with one of our coaches.

Financial abuse

- **1800RESPECT** – 1800 737 732.
- **Good Shepherd Australia Financial Independence Hub** – 1300 050 150.
- Reach out to your bank as they can be very understanding when it comes to financial abuse.

Super

- **YourSuper** – government super fund comparison tool to see how yours is performing.
- **Super Fierce** – get a free report to see if you're paying too much in fees.
- Check if you have any lost super to claim – head over to myGov.
- All superfunds have financial advisors so book a free appointment with yours.

Savings

- Compare electricity and gas deals at **Energy Made Easy**.
- **PetrolSpy** – fuel price comparison site.
- **Fuel Check NSW** – NSW fuel price comparison site.
- **ShopFully** – find your local best deals.
- **Moneysmart** – government-run financial education resource site.

Courses

- Ladies Finance Club – Investing in the Share Market For Beginners.
- Ladies Finance Club – Budget Like a Boss.
- Ladies FInance Club – Money.

Acknowledgements

To my family: Mum and Dad, thank you for always trying to get me to budget and for teaching me about investing (although I didn't listen for a long time) as well as for the endless support and encouragement that has never faded.

My incredible sisters – the loves of my life and my best friends. My twin, Rhianna, for all your endless hours of proofreading and encouragement. And my sister Briony for carrying me to the finishing line, all the LOLs and stepping me through the whole process (quick plug she's written a great book – check her out on Instagram @briony_benjamin).

Thank you to all the wonderful strong women who helped contribute to this book and have been big supporters of Ladies Finance Club and our mission from the get-go! Lisa Simpson, Lisa Conway Hughes, Meggie Palmer, Helen Francis, Katie Bryan, Emma Kirk, Christina Hobbs, Simonne Gnessen, Danielle Ecuyer, Gemma Mitchell, Trenna Probe, Tessa Kelman, Eleanor Lau, Marnie Maloney, Julia Crockett, Bernadette Janson, Samantha Lewis, Shaya Lewis-Dermody, Sarah King, Lucy Percy, Sukhy Bansal, Gemma Dale, Ellie Fordham, Andrea Jenkins, Emma Stephens, Lexi Smith, Victoria Berry, Tracey Plowman, Rachel White, Rachel O'Connor, Betsy Westcott, Jodi Petersen, Cherelle Murphy, Grace Bowe, Belinda White, Rebecca Tunstall, Effie Zahos, Helen Chong, Rory Cunningham, Julia Lee, Caroline Brewin, Jess Bardy, Christie Whitehill, Lucy Dean, Felicity Ward, Candice Bourke and Kristen Hartnett, plus the many other women who have supported us. Without you there would be no Ladies Finance Club!

My wonderful team: Lana, Mary, Abby, Anna, Trixie and Rubie.

To my incredible coaches and mentors, Dale Beaumont, Tina Tower, Michelle Broadbent and Kimberly Winters. Thank you for all that you do.

Thanks to my best pals, Lauren Stockholm, Claire Anderson, Angie Berkhout, Alice Andrewartha, Tess Law, Kristen Grimley, Victoria Smith and Andrew Cooney for being the most supportive friends, pouring the champs at events and coming along to everything when I first started out!

And finally to all the women out there who are empowering women all around them: we can do this, we have to do this – keep fighting the good fight!